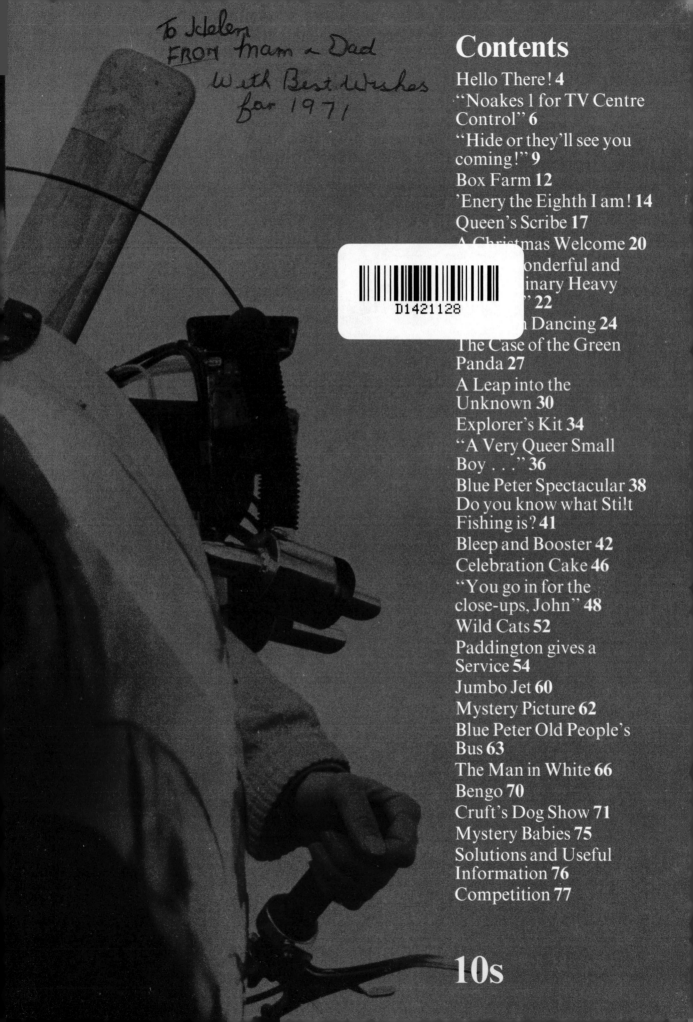

To Helen
FROM Mam & Dad
With Best Wishes
for 1971

Contents

10s

Hello There!

Here's our seventh Blue Peter Book, and it's really been very difficult to write! That's because we like our Blue Peter Books to record the highlights of what we've been doing throughout the year, and this time there seems to have been more to choose from than ever before.

But judging from your letters, the things you've enjoyed most have been *our* favourites too, so that's helped us quite a lot. And we've also been very grateful for all your suggestions for our Blue Peter Mini Books. This year we've written four new ones, and they're all about the things you specially asked for—there's the Book of Presents, the Book of Guide Dogs, the Book of Daniel, and our Expedition to Ceylon. We'll be doing some more as soon as we can, so please go on sending your ideas, because they help us to know what you like best.

One exciting thing about being on Blue Peter is that we're never really sure what's going to happen next. One minute we'll be on a nature walk with Grahame Dangerfield and the next we're hundreds of feet up a craggy peak in a raging blizzard with the R.A.F. Mountain Rescue team— or learning the Paso Doble, or

Do you recognise any of these photographs? They've all been in Blue Peter. Turn to the end for the answers.

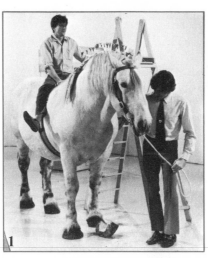

2

3

1

4

6

5

how to be a News cameraman, or piloting a gyro-glider, or finding out what actors have to do to make themselves look like Henry VIII. You can read about all these things in our book, and lots more besides. And there are things to make and stories about Bleep and Booster and Paddington, a six-clue challenge, and a brand-new competition, too.

Page 63 is very important. Here you can see exactly how we were able to aid hundreds of house-bound, lonely old people because of all the toy cars and brass plugs you sent us to buy our Old People's Buses. Once again

you've helped magnificently and you should feel very proud!

1970 has been a great year for anniversaries and we've decided to celebrate some of them. Not just the well-known ones like Charles Dickens or the founding of the Red Cross, but also the birth of a man who weighed 52 stones 11 lbs. And if you find that colossal weight a bit difficult to imagine—look at us wearing his trousers on page 22—they gave us quite a shock!

We hope you enjoy our seventh Blue Peter Book—and don't forget the competition!

Valerie Singleton

John Noakes.

Patch   Petra

Jason   Peter Purves

7

8

9

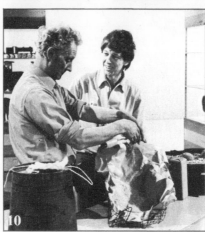

10

11

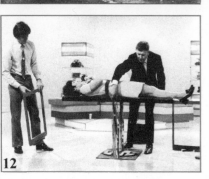

12

13

5

"Noakes 1 for TV Centre Control.
I'm coming in to land on the roof of the Blue Peter Studio – over."

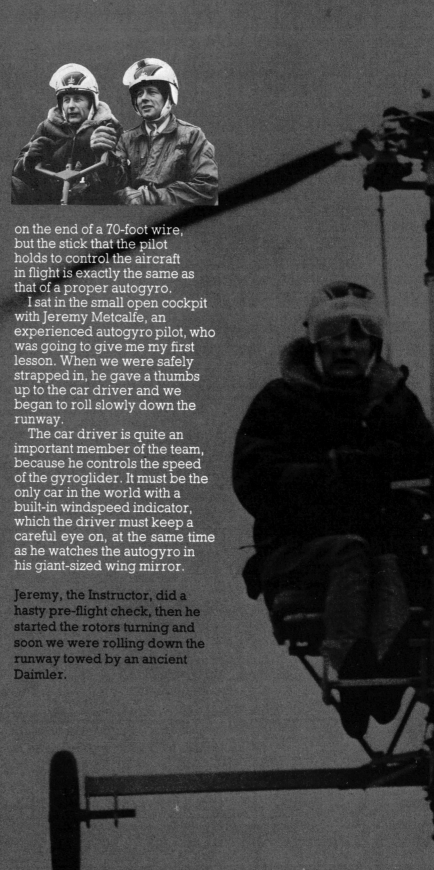

I live about 50 miles' drive from the Blue Peter Studio. Most of the journey is on a motorway, and if I went to work on a Sunday morning, I could get there in about an hour. But I always have to make the journey on Monday morning when the traffic is really terrible. The longest it's ever taken is 2½ hours – Peter and Val were furious when I arrived, and I won't tell you what Biddy Baxter said !

As I sat motionless in the traffic jam, I thought how marvellous it would be if, instead of a car, I had my own private plane that would land on the roof of the Blue Peter Studio at the Tele-vision Centre.

It could be sooner than you think.

You can get an autogyro (like one of those on the front of the book) that's 11 feet long and can fly at 90 miles an hour at a height of 11,000 feet. It does 21 miles to the gallon, needs only a 90-yard runway to get air-borne, and it doesn't cost much more than a family saloon.

What's the catch, then ? Why doesn't everybody have one ?

I was told that there are a lot of complicated reasons, one of them being that autogyro flying is quite a tricky business, so to find out more about it I went to visit a tiny airfield in Berkshire.

Every autogyro pilot begins his training on a gyroglider. It looks very similar to an auto-gyro, with one big difference – there's no engine. It's towed along the runway by a motor car on the end of a 70-foot wire, but the stick that the pilot holds to control the aircraft in flight is exactly the same as that of a proper autogyro.

I sat in the small open cockpit with Jeremy Metcalfe, an experienced autogyro pilot, who was going to give me my first lesson. When we were safely strapped in, he gave a thumbs up to the car driver and we began to roll slowly down the runway.

The car driver is quite an important member of the team, because he controls the speed of the gyroglider. It must be the only car in the world with a built-in windspeed indicator, which the driver must keep a careful eye on, at the same time as he watches the autogyro in his giant-sized wing mirror.

Jeremy, the Instructor, did a hasty pre-flight check, then he started the rotors turning and soon we were rolling down the runway towed by an ancient Daimler.

Jeremy pulled the starting cord of a small two-stroke motor which began to revolve the rotor blades, but as soon as they were moving the motor was cut and the blades were kept turning by wind alone.

The car began to gather speed, and soon the nose wheel started to lift from the ground – and we were airborne.

Jeremy showed me how to pull back the stick to climb, push it forward to go down, and move it to the right and left for turning.

It all sounds terribly simple, but the aircraft responds to the smallest movement, and you've got to move the stick very gently to avoid turning the whole thing over.

Jeremy brought the gyro-glider down for a perfect landing, the car slowed down and then turned back up the runway to tow us back to our starting position. I'd felt quite

happy holding the stick with Jeremy's hand reassuringly guiding mine to make the correct movements, but the moment of truth came when Jeremy hopped from the cockpit and said :

"Right, John. You're on your own now. Just give the car a thumbs up sign when you're ready to go."

"You're joking," I said.

"No – you'll be all right. Keep your eyes on the horizon – and don't jerk the stick whatever you do !"

I gave a somewhat hesitant thumbs up sign, and started to move slowly along the tarmac.

I could hear the swish-swish of the rotor blades as I gathered speed, and I watched the nose wheel, waiting for it to rear up in front of me. Gradually we increased speed, and then, very slowly, the nose wheel began to lift. I pushed the stick slightly forward to balance the aircraft, then eased it gently back, and up I soared into the air.

Below me I could see the car dead ahead of me on the runway. I moved the stick to the left and swung out in a glorious soaring movement over the field by the side of the tarmac. I now had the car on my right and I could see the end of the runway ahead. I thought I'd better not try anything too spectacular, so I eased the stick to the right, and the aircraft slewed obediently back over the runway.

Forward with the stick – down

We started to gather speed and the nose-wheel began to lift off the ground—forward with the stick to balance the aircraft, then gently back as we soared into the air. This was my first flight with an instructor. I didn't know it at the time, but my next flight was going to be solo!

I came – and with only the slightest bump I was safely back on the tarmac again.

I felt quite pleased with myself as I stepped out of the cockpit, and Jeremy said I hadn't done too badly for a first attempt.

As I got back into my car, I looked longingly at the tiny autogyro at the end of the runway, and I thought of all the traffic jams between me and home. It was just coming up for the rush hour, too.

Mind you, have you thought what it would be like if everybody had one?

Last year there were more than 100,000 accidents on the London streets alone. Some of them weren't serious, but if everyone had been flying autogyros instead of driving cars, they'd have been falling from the skies like confetti.

"Hide, or they'll see you coming!"

That's what Grahame Danger-field said to me one freezing winter morning as we set out to look for wild animals, and that's why I found myself sitting half-way up a tree, hardly daring to breathe as the animals drew closer and closer.

When we first set out on our expedition, I didn't think we had a chance of seeing anything! Our feet were sinking deep in snow, the temperature was only a couple of degrees off freezing point, and it seemed to me that any animal with sense would be tucked up somewhere warm! But Grahame explained that a day like this was ideal for animal-spotting, and for a very good reason.

We were hardly making a sound as we walked across the fields towards the stream. No twigs were snapping, no leaves were rustling–we were silent as Indians as our boots sank up to the ankles in the thick snow. No animals would get warning of our approach, so if we were careful we had a good chance of getting quite close to them.

Grahame pointed out that it wasn't only *our* footprints that were showing up in the snow. Lots of birds and animals have to come out to look for food whatever the weather, and if we kept our eyes open, we'd be able to spot their tracks.

"Look!" said Grahame, pointing to some footprints in the snow. "What do you think those are?"

"Could be a dog," I said. "Petra leaves prints like that."

"Could be," said Grahame, "but I don't think so. The snow's fallen in on the prints, so they're not too clear, but I'm pretty sure it's a fox. You can see where he's walked along the stream and turned round. He's probably just sniffing along the bank looking for duck. But there's some other prints here I want you to have a look at. I wonder if you know what these are?"

I knelt down in the snow and took a close look.

"It looks like a cattle hoofmark–a cow or something–but it's too small. Is it a deer?"

"Right!" said Grahame. "It's the print of a Roe Deer. There are quite a lot of them living round this area. I've got a hide near here, so if you like we could go there for a bit and if we're very lucky, we might see them come down to the stream. Do you want to come?"

Of course I wanted to! I'd never seen wild Roe Deer, and this was too good a chance to miss.

We walked on for a few minutes until we came to the tree where Grahame had built his hide. There was a metal ladder already in position, and my hands just about froze to the icy rungs as I followed Grahame up. The hide itself wasn't exactly luxurious! It was just an old door wedged firmly into the spreading branches with some sacking spread round to make flimsy walls about three feet high.

"Deer don't usually look upwards," explained Grahame, "so they're not likely to see us anyway. But just in case they do, the sacking disguises the human outline. If we're just peeping over the top, they won't see us. All we've got to do now is wait and hope they'll turn up."

You need a lot of patience to be a naturalist and after about forty minutes of sitting on a door in the snow without moving or talking, I was beginning to wonder if I had enough! It was getting colder and colder, and I was feeling like a solid block of ice when Grahame suddenly gave me a little nudge.

Cautiously I peered over the sacking, and there was a marvellous sight! About twenty yards away a pair of Roe Deer were just breaking cover through the bushes. They were beautiful to

look at, and their soft brown coats stood out sharply against the dazzling white snow. Now I was glad I'd come animal spotting in the winter, for in the spring and summer the Roe Deer's natural camouflage makes them difficult to spot against the leaves and fields.

"They're just about fully grown," Grahame whispered to me. "They're last year's babies."

"How can you tell?" I whispered back.

"Just by the whole look of them. You see the male? He's got little horns. It's the start of his antlers, and they're still covered in what's called velvet! That means they've still got skin over them. He'll rub this off soon and expose the bare horn."

"Will they grow bigger?" I whispered.

"Not much," Grahame whispered back, "but quiet now. They're coming closer!"

I watched breathlessly as the little deer drew nearer and nearer. Just as Grahame had predicted, they never looked up once. They walked right underneath our hide, nuzzling in the snow for food and leaving prints all round the tree just like the ones Grahame had shown me in the field. I was really enjoying watching them when, suddenly, it happened!

"Atishoo!" I let out the most enormous sneeze. I tried not to, but I simply couldn't help it! At once the deer's heads shot up, nervously they looked quickly round, and in one bound they were away. They shot into the bushes and disappeared for good!

"Never mind," said Grahame. "We did get a look at them, and it's time we were getting home anyway."

Back at his house, Grahame took me to see Foxy, who lived in a pen at the bottom of the garden. He was a magnificent-looking beast in beautiful condition, and he owed his life to Grahame. He'd been found lying in the road one day, badly hurt by a car, and someone had brought him to Grahame to look after. But now he was cured Grahame had decided to let him go.

"He's quite able to fend for himself now, Peter," said Grahame. "Let's take him to the common and let him go."

"Isn't it a bit late?" I said. "It's almost dark."

"That's why I want to release him now," replied Grahame. "It'll give him the whole night to settle down in the wild. You see, no one will bother him at night. He can creep about in the dark and sort himself out."

Grahame picked Foxy up by the scruff of the neck and held him tightly in his arms.

"I have to hold him like this," he said, as we walked to the common. "He'd bite me as soon as look at me. He's not a bit tame!"

Even though Grahame had been looking after him every day, Foxy certainly hadn't become a pet. As Grahame said, it was high time he got back to the wild. And Foxy couldn't wait.

"This looks a good place, Peter," said Grahame as we reached the common, and he put Foxy on the ground. He was gone in a flash–streaking across the snow and heading for cover. He was on his way home and ready to join all the hundreds of other wild animals that there are in Britain–rabbits, hares, badgers and dozens of other breeds that are there to be spotted if you use your eyes and have plenty of patience.

11

Box Farm

If you would like a farm-house to complete your farm set, here's an idea for making one from two shoe boxes. There's a real door that opens, see-through windows made from cellophane, a porch made from a shallow box, and for a finishing touch, I've thatched the roof with raffia.

1 It's easiest to make the porch and doorway first. Draw a door shape on a small cardboard box or box lid, and cut along three sides. Leave one long side uncut so that the door can be opened.

2 Put the porch on one side of a shoe box and draw round it. Next, cut out the card about half an inch inside the lines you've drawn and bend the card that's left outwards along the lines.

3 Draw in the windows and cut them out. It's a good idea to cut a piece of card for a pattern so that all the windows will be the same size. Glue the porch firmly in place and leave it to dry.

4 Next, paint the house. I've used emulsion paint, but any un-shiny paint will do. When the paint's dry, stick pieces of cellophane inside the box to make the windows. If you cut the cellophane bigger than you need, it's easier to stick in place, and the extra bit won't be seen from the outside. I've used strips of sticky plastic for the panes and match-sticks for the frames.

5 To make the front door look real, cover the front with wood-grained plastic or coloured paper. Then push a brass paper fastener through to make a door knob. Make a roof for the porch from a little piece of card with strips of raffia glued on to make the thatch. Glue it into place.

6 For the roof, use a second shoe box. Cut down in a sloping line from the corners and then cut along the bottom of the box and you will have a roof shape that fits the house. Thatch the roof with raffia, or real straw if you can get it. Paint the sides of the roof to match the house.

7 Make a chimney from a piece of a cardboard box that toothpaste has been packed in. All you have to do is cut a V-shape in each side so that it fits on to the roof. Paint the chimney, and when it's dry, mark in the bricks with a black pen or pencil.

8 If you've got two more smaller boxes, you could make a little cottage to go with the farm. The boxes don't have to be the same size as each other, but here's a useful tip. Keep the biggest box for the roof, or your cottage won't look right !

'Enery the Eighth I am!

Do you recognise these pictures? They're both of King Henry VIII—but one is Hans Holbein's famous portrait, and the other is that well-known star of television—John Noakes!

In the days before photography was invented, portrait painters were very important men, and 400 years ago, the most famous of them all was Hans Holbein. Holbein—a German—was one of the best portrait painters of his day. His fame spread far and wide and King Henry VIII asked him to come to England to paint him and his court and family. It's thanks to Holbein that we know what people like Henry's Court Jester, and his daughter, Mary Tudor, and his wives, Anne Boleyn and Anne of Cleeves, looked like and what they wore. And there's one painting above all that people remember—Holbein's portrait of Henry himself.

But little did Holbein know that hundreds of years later this picture would be so well known it would be the cause of a tricky problem, because nowadays, any actor who plays the part of Henry VIII on stage, or on television, or in a film, must look *exactly* like the portrait. And that means not only wearing elaborate make-up, but also some very uncomfortable clothes.

Fortunately, the BBC's Make-up and Wardrobe Departments are used to solving problems—even when they're asked to transform a slim, clean-shaven John Noakes into a fat, bearded king.

The day I decided to see what it was like to be Henry VIII is one

I certainly won't forget in a hurry. It took me over half an hour to get the costume on, and two hours to have my false hair put on and my face made up! Here's a behind-the-scenes view of how the transformation took place:

1 To start with, my hair was the wrong colour and there was too much of it. So it was smoothed under this semi-transparent bladder to give me a receding hair line.

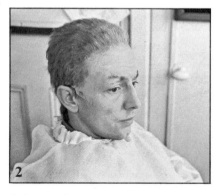

2 A red wig came next—to match the colour and shape of Henry's hair.

3 After my false beard and moustache had been carefully arranged, and my large, feather-trimmed hat placed at the right angle, I had to stuff cheek padding in my mouth to fatten out my face. This was extraordinarily uncomfortable and made it very difficult to speak properly. But if I'd been going to play the part of Henry on stage or in a film, I would have had the padding moulded on to the *outside* of my face, and then skilfully covered by make-up.

4 Jo Young, Make-up Supervisor, adjusted the royal beard—and I practised the royal frown.

5 Jo and I compared my make-up with Holbein's portrait—so far I felt the likeness was pretty convincing, and Jo was pleased too.

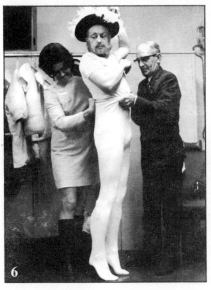

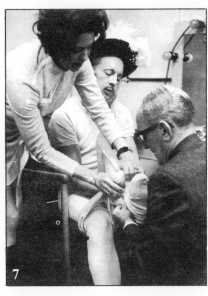

6 Costume Supervisor, Jane Nagy, and Wardrobe Master, David Wears, took over. The Royal under-garments began with a very large pair of long woollen pants!

7 Next came a struggle with my overtights, into which were inserted two special bits of padding called symmetricals, to give me shapely royal calves.

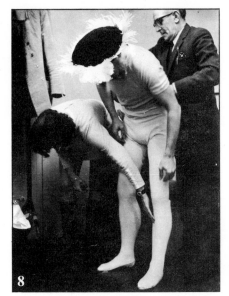

8 Jane made sure my symmetricals weren't slipping!

9 My body padding began with this thick jacket. The jacket was made rather like a vest with the back and the front padded out with a load of old wadding. And underneath was a T-shirt which had been cut right down the back. This meant I could get the jacket on quite easily without dragging it over my head and disturbing my wig and beard and the rest of my make-up. By now I was so hot, I'd been allowed to take off my hat.

10 But worse was to come—my temperature was going to rise even higher with the next garment I had to wear. A second, even more enormous jacket with a built-in Henry-shaped tummy was fitted over the first one—this too was padded and was even

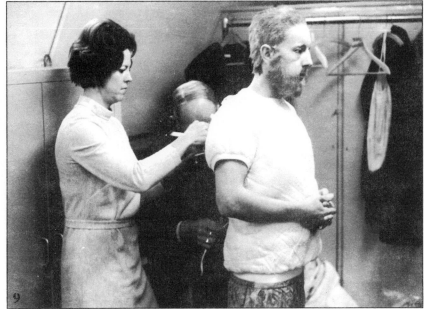

hotter than the under-jacket. Inside it felt as though I was back in that Sauna bath I once had.

11 My tunic was fastened with dozens of hooks and eyes, just as Henry's had been 400 years earlier.

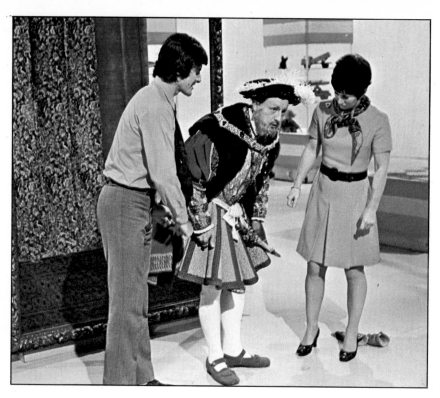

12 Val and Pete helped me with the finishing touches. A heavy surcoat with a fur collar. A chain and pendant made of links, each inscribed with an H for Henry. A dagger, sheath and two belts, to say nothing of my gloves, a purple garter and my royal shoes.

It was two and a half hours since I'd been fitted with my semi-transparent bladder, but even though I felt ready to drop with heat and exhaustion, I had to admit it was well worth all the trouble. I really felt like a King!

And it's strange to think that it's all because of Holbein's famous four-hundred-year-old portrait that actors have to go through such agony whenever they play the part of Henry VIII.

Queen's Scribe

"Elizabeth the Second by the Grace of God of the United Kingdom of Great Britain and Northern Ireland and of Our other Realms and Territories Queen Head of the Commonwealth Defender of the Faith…"

These words come from the Letters Patent given by Queen Elizabeth II to the Prince of Wales during his Investiture. It was really a letter from the Queen introducing Prince Charles to the people. Without it, Charles could not have been created Prince of Wales, and this meant it was a vital part of the Ceremony.

Proclamations like this have to be hand-written by a scribe, and in the whole of Britain there are only two scribes who write Letters Patent for the Queen. One of them is Donald Jackson, and I took Blue Peter cameras to visit him in his Camberwell Studio to see exactly how he did his beautiful lettering and how he decorates his manuscripts.

Donald has other patrons as well as the Queen, because anyone who can afford it can commission a scribe to write for him. On one wall was pinned a vast family tree that he was designing for an American family. Another American – an oil millionaire – had commissioned an elaborately decorated map of Texas. Donald was just about to add a few Red Indians brandishing tomahawks, and I began to realise that a scribe does far more than just lettering. He has to be able to draw and paint as well. And what was particularly fascinating was that Donald was using the same sort of writing

1 The Queen hands the Letters Patent to the Prince of Wales during the Investiture. They were written and decorated by a scribe.

2 This detail shows the fine workmanship in another Letters Patent. A scribe must be able to draw and paint as well as write – in 500 years the colours will look as brilliant as they do today.

3 Donald Jackson, one of the Queen's Scribes, showed me how to cut a quill. He uses the same materials as the medieval scribes.

4 Stripping the quill. If the barbs were left on, the scribe would tickle his chin as he wrote.

5 A razor-sharp knife is used to cut the nib. This quill comes from one of the Queen's own swans.

materials and paints as the monks used 500 years earlier when they were making their beautiful copies of the Bible.

To show me exactly how he worked, Donald said he'd do a special scroll for Blue Peter with our ship designed in glittering gold leaf.

But first he had to do the lettering, and for this Donald writes with a quill. You can use a fountain pen with interchangeable lettering nibs, but Donald says there's nothing better than a quill. They have to be made from goose, turkey, or swan's wing feathers, and Donald was lucky – his feathers had come from one of the Queen's swans.

I'd never seen a quill cut before – and here came my first surprise – proper scribes strip off the barbs or feathery bits so that they don't get tickled

under their chins when they write. The quill is then cut to a comfortable length, and the nib is squared and shaped, with a slit in the centre to feed the ink to the tip. Donald used a fantastically sharp knife – rather like a doctor's scalpel – to cut the quill, and it was sharpened so that the blade followed the curve of the pen. For perfect writing, the edges of the nib must be sharp and clean.

Donald's ink didn't come from a bottle. It was Chinese Stick ink – a solidified mixture of gum and soot. The ink was made liquid by rubbing the stick in a tiny saucer filled with rain water.

Vellum, or calf's skin, is still the finest material in the world to write on. (Parchment, or sheep's skin, is much coarser.) But great care must be taken not to get grease on the surface

of the vellum, as this will prevent the ink from running smoothly. Even a finger print will spoil the surface, so Donald uses a silk handkerchief for a handrest.

I held my breath as he made the first strokes. There was the wide, fat curve of the ''B'' – then an elegant, thin twist to the loop of the ''L'' as he began to write ''Blue Peter''. And surprisingly the strokes were made thick or thin not by the pressure put on the nib, but by altering the *angle* at which it was held. It seemed so effortless and so fast, I could scarcely believe my eyes. Donald's ''Blue Peter'' – more beautifully written than I had ever seen it before – had taken him precisely five seconds!

Many of the manuscripts Donald writes are decorated in a bright glowing red – and

6 Thick and thin strokes are made not by pressure, but by altering the *angle* of the pen. The silk handkerchief is used as a handrest to protect the vellum from grease.

7 Pricking the yolk of an egg to separate it from its skin. Egg yolk gives the red paint a bright and luminous sheen.

8 The yolk is mixed with a cake of vermilion colouring and some rain water to form the red paint.

9 The gold leaf is put on a suede gilder's cushion, and cut into squares with another sharp knife. Again, grease is a danger so the knife must be clean.

10 By blowing down this tube, Donald moistens the sails which have been painted in a kind of paste called gesso, and the gold is made to stick. All that needs to be done now is to burnish the gold leaf.

11 Our own special "Blue Peter" scroll – designed and decorated by a Queen's Scribe.

again, this is paint he mixes himself. We were going to have 1970 written in red on our "Blue Peter" scroll, and for this, Donald needed an egg. It sounded more like cooking than painting – especially when the yolk had to be carefully separated from the white.

Then, very delicately, Donald pierced the skin of the yolk with his scalpel, and let the yolk pour into a saucer. Into this he mixed a cake of vermilion colouring in just the same way as the Chinese Stick ink. A few drops of rain water were added, and the paint was ready.

Donald said that the yolk of egg would make the red paint dry with a brilliant luminous sheen that would last for hundreds of years. And you only have to look at decorated medieval manuscripts to see how right he is.

I was interested to see that Donald didn't waste his egg whites. The one he'd just separated from the yolk was going to be added to his gesso – a kind of paste that's used as a foundation for gold leaf.

Donald had painted our "Blue Peter" ship in gesso and it was to be covered in gold. Gold leaf is bought by the bookful – and the leaves are so thin a bee's breath would blow them away. Carefully, Donald spread one of the wafer-thin sheets of gold leaf on to his suede gilder's cushion. Then he cut it into squares using a long, flat knife.

Again, grease is a danger. It's important the knife is completely grease-free, so Donald kept his fingers off the blade.

Bits of gold were placed gently on to the outline of the ship, and the next stage was quite remarkable. Donald put a

tube into his mouth and blew on to the sails. The blowing moistened the sugar in the gesso which made the gold stick.

After that, all that was left was to burnish the gold leaf. This meant gently rubbing it until it shone so brightly it was almost too dazzling to look at. (Manuscripts were said to be "illuminated" because of the brightness of the gold.)

Now we had our own "Blue Peter" scroll, decorated by a real craftsman. In 500 years' time the red and the gold will look as vivid and brilliant as they do today.

And just as today we keep medieval manuscripts in museums, it's strange to think that in the year 2470 our scroll may well be treasured as a valuable collector's item!

A Christmas Welcome

A decorated door looks specially
welcoming at Christmas-time, so
if you're making decorations, why
not hang one outside for everyone
to see?
My decoration is made from a
polystyrene ceiling tile, a string of
tinsel, a cake doyley, some pieces
of ribbon and a bit of holly. It's
cheap and quick to make, and if
you pack it away carefully, it will
last for years. Here's how to
make it:

1 First of all, fix a string of gold tinsel right round the ceiling tile. Start at one corner by pushing a pin first through the tinsel and then firmly into the side of the tile. One pin at each corner is quite sufficient to hold the tinsel firmly in place.

2 Glue a gold cake doyley to the centre of the tile. Some types of glue melt polystyrene, so it's a good idea to check your glue first by putting a dab at the back of the tile. I found that rubber solution glue was very good. It doesn't spoil the tile, and if you make a mistake, it's easy to rub off and start again.

3 I used holly sprays to finish off the centre of the decoration. Mine's plastic, but if you can get real holly, it looks even better. Push the stems right through the ceiling tile and bend them flat at the back. A few strips of sticky tape will hold them neatly in place.

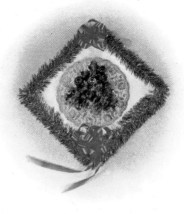

4 Make two bows, one for the top and one for the bottom of the decoration. I've used red gift ribbon, the kind that sticks to itself when moistened. Just make a loop, and where the strips meet, moisten and press together. On one bow, I've left two long ends as they look good hanging down the door.

5 For the finishing touches, pin or glue the small bow to the top corner and the big bow to the bottom, and add some small coloured balls. To hang the decoration, thread a loop of thin wire through the top point of the tile

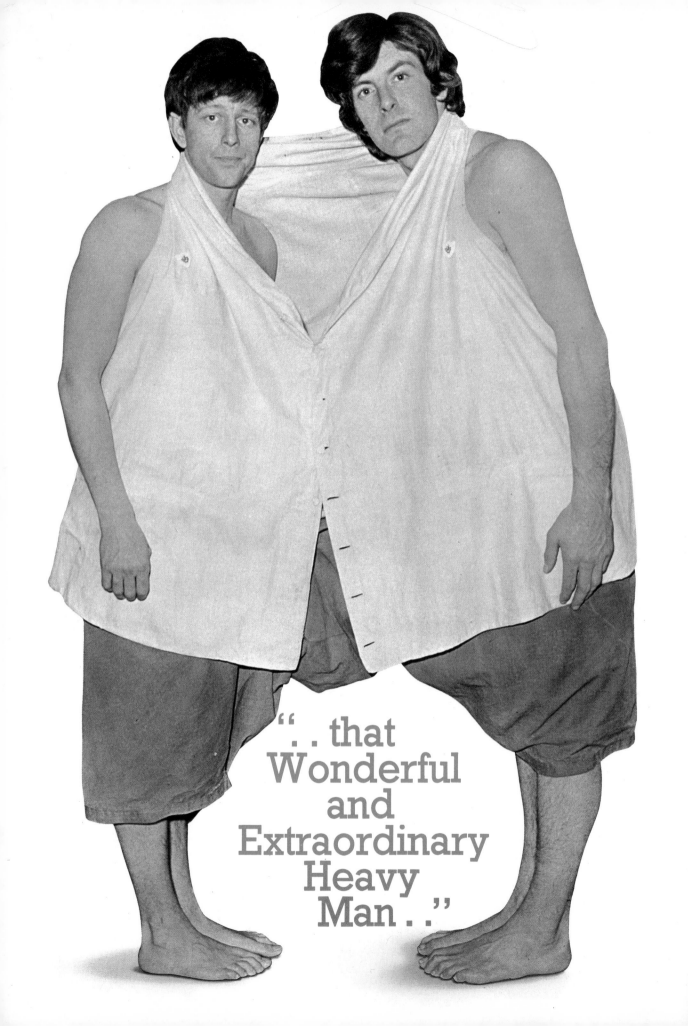

"..that Wonderful and Extraordinary Heavy Man.."

Daniel Lambert: Height 5' 11" Waist 9' 4" Weight 52 stone 11 lbs.

Imagine weighing 52 stone 11 lbs! When we first heard about Daniel Lambert, we could hardly believe our ears – it's quite difficult to imagine a man with a waist measurement of 9 feet 4 inches. But these were Daniel Lambert's vital statistics, and as 1970 was his 200th anniversary, we decided we'd visit Leicester's Newarke Houses Museum, where we could actually see the very clothes he wore and lots of his personal possessions.

And we weren't disappointed. We were given special permission to try on his gigantic trousers, and when we found we could each stand inside one trouser leg with ample room to spare, we began to realise what it must have been like to be one of the only two Britons with a recorded weight of more than 50 stone.

Of course, being so huge could have been a terrible handicap, but Daniel Lambert was far from downhearted. He was a keen sportsman and rode a famous horse called Monarch – the largest horse in the world – who stood over 21 hands – and that's over 7 feet! They must have been a pretty impressive pair – which was probably why they were drawn in a political cartoon with Daniel in military uniform riding Monarch and towering over a small and shrinking Napoleon.

Daniel enjoyed walking and you can see two of his walking-sticks at the Newarke Houses. He was also a good swimmer and gave lessons to the local children, who were allowed to use his massive back as a diving-board as he lay obligingly on his tummy.

After working as an apprentice engraver and a breeder of terriers, Daniel became a gaoler at the Bridewell Prison, where he was held in great affection by the prisoners. When it closed in 1805, he decided he would have to earn his living by exhibiting himself to the public, charging an entrance fee of a shilling.

So in 1806 he travelled to London in a coach that had to be specially built for him, and took rooms at 53 Piccadilly. But instead of turning into a cheap sideshow, Daniel began to gain a reputation as a great wit – and woe betide visitors who were impertinent. When a woman was rude enough to ask the price of his coat, he replied:

"If you think proper to make me a present of a new coat, you will then know exactly what it costs."

Later on, Daniel travelled to several other towns, and it was when he was visiting Stamford for the races that he died at the age of 39.

The only way his body could be taken from the ground-floor room of the Waggon and Horses Inn where he was staying was by knocking the wall down. His coffin had to be built on wheels and more than twenty men were needed to lower it into his grave.

No one knows why Daniel Lambert grew so large. He was a teetotaller and not at all greedy, so it is thought his fatness was due to a disease. But although he was so heavy – more than twice the weight of the three of us together – he was never in any pain.

His tombstone is an unusual one because it gives his measurements. But if you think that Daniel Lambert holds the world record – you're wrong! Robert Hughes of Missouri beats him by 22 stone 8 lbs – just try imagining the size of *his* trousers!

As Daniel's fame spread, he became the subject for cartoonists. This one is called "The Wonders of the World, or a Specimen of a New Troop of Leicestershire Light Horse". The cringing Napoleon cries, "If dis be de specimen of de English Light Horse, vat vill de Heavy Horse be! I vill put of de Invasion for an oder time!"

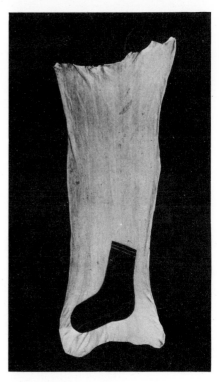

John's sock is nine times smaller than Daniel's stocking. Daniel's calf measurement was 3' 1" – John's is 9 inches!

I've never had a ballroom dancing lesson in my life, but I've watched "Come Dancing" on television and seen all those chaps got up in white tie and tails with numbers on their backs, gliding about in a spotlight with girls dressed in 80 yards of net covered in thousands of sequins. It didn't look all that difficult, so full of confidence I went to meet World Champion Peggy Spencer in her ballroom at Penge.

Peggy, a tall, statuesque lady (she was a couple of inches taller than me), began by teaching me a special quickstep.

When you start learning ballroom dancing, you put both hands on your instructor's shoulders, so that you leave a gap big enough to allow you to look down and see what your feet are doing. My feet were my greatest problem! Peggy said my steps looked as though I was wearing "seven-league boots". Ballroom dancing steps have to be short and precise.

"Now we'll try the chassé," said Peggy. "Do you know what a chassé is?"

"Part of a motor car?"

"Not in ballroom dancing," she said.

With my arms on Peggy's shoulders, I could look down to see what my feet were doing.

It was a sort of half skip, which makes you change step and lead off with the other foot.

"Now we come to the bit where you feature the girl. It's called a Polka turn. You go through on your right foot – slow – and as you step to the side on your left foot, you've got to turn your body to the right."

I'm not very good on my lefts and rights in the first place, but now she was asking me to walk one way and turn to face the other.

"Your body's all right, but your feet are in a terrible muddle!"

As ballroom dancing is the art of moving your feet in time to music, I felt I wasn't doing very well.

We staggered on and I was shown the intricacies of *Pendulum Point*, *The Skid*, *Promenade Point*, and the *Woodpecker Tap*. Eventually, Peggy said:

"How about doing it in hold?"

That meant doing it close together in a clinch like proper dancers, so there'd be no chance of looking at my feet. This was pretty difficult, but my problems really started when Peggy said:

"Right – we'll do it to music."

To a scratchy gramophone record, playing in strict tempo, we moved off with Peggy calling the time over the music.

Whilst I was learning the quickstep, Val was having a quick refresher course with Frank Spencer, Peggy's husband, who was also a world champion ballroom dancer. Val had learnt ballroom dancing when she was a little girl, and had a chestful of gold medals to prove it. I'd had half a day to reach her standard so that we could hold our own Blue Peter Ballroom Championships. But more of that later on.

Having mastered the quickstep, which meant that I'd got round the floor without actually crippling Peggy for life, she turned to me and said:

"Would you like to learn a dance of fire?"

"Yes," I said. I couldn't think of any alternative.

"We'll have a go at the tango, then."

This is a real slinky dance – that's meant to be done with passion and Latin fervour.

At least, it was – until I tried it!

There's something about a 5' 8" Yorkshireman in a thick-knit woolly and suede boots trying to do a fiery dance with a world champion who's two inches taller than he is. I wouldn't exactly call it Latin fervour – but it's quite spectacular, believe you me!

"Step back on your left foot – gather up all your strength – turn to your left and sway down, holding me in your arms – it's called the X line."

"Is your husband watching?" I asked, nervously.

"Drop your shoulder down and come round into the contra check."

I felt like a back-to-front man – my toes were pointing one way and my head the other.

"I can't move," I gasped.

"I think you've just invented a new variation," said Peggy bravely as she slipped slowly to the floor.

When we'd finally extinguished any smouldering embers that remained of the dance of fire, I limped off to get changed. I wanted

2

3

Peggy showed me how to do
1 the Pendulum Point, 2 the
Woodpecker Tap, and 3 the
Promenade Point.

to find out what it was like to be one of those chaps on "Come Dancing".

Off came the thick-knit woolly and suede boots and on went a black tail-coat with No. 18 on the back and a gleaming pair of patent-leather shoes.

Mr John Noakes of Halifax was about to compete in the first ever Blue Peter Ballroom Championships partnered by Miss Valerie Singleton of Kensington, clad in a mile of net, sparkling with a million sequins.

Val and I slid off across the floor and stepped into a pool of light. The first few steps were all right, and I even managed the chassé quite successfully. But then I started to head for the wall and I didn't know how to get out of it.

"We're supposed to do a turn here," muttered Val in my ear.

"Mmmm?" I said, with studied nonchalance – and the wall grew bigger and bigger.

"I'll tell you what – let's stop and start again – nobody's watching," hissed Val.

We had about four false starts, but the final indignity came when the music ended with a flourish but we carried on and did a couple of chassés and a pendulum point in deadly silence.

My favourite bit was the Paso Doble. For this, I changed again and wore a cutaway coat, frilly front and a flat Spanish hat. Val wore a shorter, red, frilly dress. The Paso Doble is supposed to simulate the action of the Matador and the Bull at a Bull fight. I was the Matador – and Val (for some reason that I can't quite figure out) was the bull.

The dance ends with a tableau when the girl (being the bull) kneels on one knee, and the fellow stands on tiptoe with his arms raised up over his head in a big Spanish gesture.

For a second, I really felt the part – until that rotten Valerie Singleton stretched out her hands and tickled me in the ribs, which put an end to my Latin fervour.

The event was over, and as No. 18 were the only couple competing, No. 18 – Mr J. Noakes of Halifax and Miss V. Singleton of Kensington – were voted outright winners of the first and (we hope) the last Blue Peter Ballroom Dancing Championships.

I joined Miss Valerie Singleton of Kensington for the Blue Peter Ballroom Championships of 1969. Val and I slid across the floor and stepped into a pool of light. My favourite bit was the Paso Doble. I was supposed to be a bull-fighter, and Val (for some strange reason!) was the bull.

The Case of the Green Panda

Bob McCann was delighted! He'd got a marvellous job for the holidays. He was an Assistant Keeper at Lord Foxborough's private zoo on his country estate at Villiers.

When Bob arrived for work one Saturday morning, he found Lord Foxborough in a high state of excitement.

"Bob, I want you to get the special cage ready. This morning I've had news of an exciting new arrival. It will be the pride of my collection!"

"What sort of animal is it?" asked Bob.

"It's one of the rarest in the world–a Giant Panda!"

"Gosh!" exclaimed Bob. "However have you managed that?"

"It's all here, in this cable from my friend Sing Li Tong."

"Sing Li Who?" questioned Bob.

"He's one of my oldest friends," explained Foxborough. "I saved his life in the uprising in '26, and he was so grateful he said he'd give me anything I desired. Sing Li Tong is an extremely rich man, but when I said all I really wanted was a panda, he knew that I had asked for something that money couldn't buy, because a panda is the rarest animal in the world. Nevertheless an

Eastern gentleman always keeps his promise, so he gave me that priceless *jade* panda that you may have seen on the desk in my study with the assurance that one day he would exchange the jade for a real, live panda."

He passed Bob the cable from China. It read:
Panda arriving 25th May with my agent Hue Wel Dhun and interpreter Sims. Return jade as arranged.

"That's today," cried Bob. "They'll be here any minute."

And even as he spoke, a black Mercedes purred up the drive and out stepped a small Chinese, and a tall, thin European.

The Chinese bowed.

"Do I have the honour of addressing Lord Foxborough?" he said. "Fliend of my master Sing Li Tong? I bling gleetings and good news, but I spik little English. My fliend Honourable Montague Sims will speak."

The tall man smiled and stepped forward.

"Morning, Lord Foxborough. Delighted to meet you."

Lord Foxborough shook him warmly by the hand. "Have you brought the panda with you?" he said. "I can't wait to see it."

"No, actually we haven't, because we wanted

to be absolutely sure you had the right accommodation for it. Hue Wel Dhun is an international expert in the care of pandas, and before we hand it over he must be sure that everything is in order."

"Of course, my dear fellow," said Lord Foxborough. "Bob, show them where we intend to keep the little creature."

As they walked through the Zoo, Hue Wel Dhun said a few whispered words in Chinese to the interpreter, who turned immediately to Bob and asked:

"What about the heaters? Hue Wel Dhun is worried that the English climate could be fatal to a tropical animal like the panda. The accommodation must be as warm as its native jungle in Tibet."

"We'll do everything we can to look after the panda," said Bob.

"You realise how much care must be taken," said Sims. "The pandas in London, Moscow and Basle Zoos are treated like gold. They are the only other pandas in captivity in Europe."

"We'll look after it all right," said Bob. "What about its food?"

Sims turned to the Chinese and exchanged a few rapid words.

"Mr Hue says he will eat mainly bran and oats, but you must cut down that overhanging bamboo tree because bamboo shoots are poisonous to pandas."

By now they'd arrived at the special cage and Bob unlocked it to show the two men round. Immediately, Mr Hue rattled the bars and looked worried.

"Panda he climb velly high. Sometime he climb light to top of Mount Fujiyama. Must make cage velly stlong!"

"We'll see to that, sir," said Bob. "Once we've got him, we don't intend to lose him."

He turned to Mr Sims.

"By the way, won't the panda have to go into quarantine before we can have him at the zoo?"

"Oh no," said Sims. "Sing Li Tong is a very important man. He has special permission from the Emperor of China himself to make this present to his friend Lord Foxborough."

As he spoke, Lord Foxborough joined them.

"Well, Bob–been looking after our guests? Be a good chap and run along and get the jade from my study. Here are the keys."

Sims and the Chinese looked at each other and smiled as Bob made off in the direction of the house. But when he got to the study he dialled 01 230 1212 and waited breathlessly for an answer.

"New Scotland Yard," came the reply.

"May I speak to Detective Sergeant McCann?" he said, urgently.

"McCann here."

"Hello Uncle," said Bob. "Can you come down here right away? I've something very important to tell you . . ."

In the meantime, the men were waiting impatiently for Bob to return with the jade. At last Bob arrived, but empty-handed.

"What's the matter, man? Where's the jade?" queried Lord Foxborough, tersely.

"I'm afraid it isn't there," blustered Bob.

"Isn't there? What do you mean, man?"

"It isn't there, sir. I've searched high and low!"

"Then call the police at once," cried Lord Foxborough.

"I already have," said Bob.

Hue Wel Dhun and Sims looked horrified.

"If the jade has been mislaid, we cannot bring the panda," barked Sims.

Hue smiled enigmatically.

"We leave now. We come back tomollow, then perhaps missing jade will have leturned."

Without another word the pair stepped back into the car and drove to the gates.

"Now what?" said Sims as he stepped on the accelerator. "Our plans are ruined!"

But Mr Hue didn't seem worried.

"Old Chinese proverb say 'What you cannot achieve by day, you may accomplish by stealth in night'." He smiled inscrutably.

That night, as the old stable clock chimed twelve and the hyenas prowled in their cages, the great sash windows of Lord Foxborough's study creaked open.

A shaft of light from a torch played about the room and came to rest on Lord Foxborough's desk. There was a sudden flash of green, and there, glittering in the darkness, was the most priceless jade carving in the world.

"The jade panda," whispered Sims. "I don't understand, it was here all the time!"

"Old Chinese proverb say 'What is invisible in noon-day sun shall be revealed in darkest night'," and Hue's delicate hand slid forward to grasp the gleaming treasure.

Suddenly the room was flooded with light.

"Old English proverb says 'What is revealed by electric light is two of the craftiest jewel thieves in the world'," rasped Detective Sergeant McCann. "Grab him Bob!"

As Sims jumped for the window, Bob lunged forward in a flying rugger tackle that brought him crashing to the ground. Simultaneously, Lord Foxborough parried Hue's karate chop and let him have a straight left on the chin.

"What I still don't understand," said Lord Foxborough, breathlessly, as McCann snapped the hand-cuffs onto the two thieves, "is why you suspected them in the first place!"

"They made six very foolish mistakes, Lord Foxborough," said Bob.

"Yes," added McCann, "and thanks to my nephew here, the case of the Green Panda can now be closed."

Did you spot the six mistakes? Check your answers on page 76.

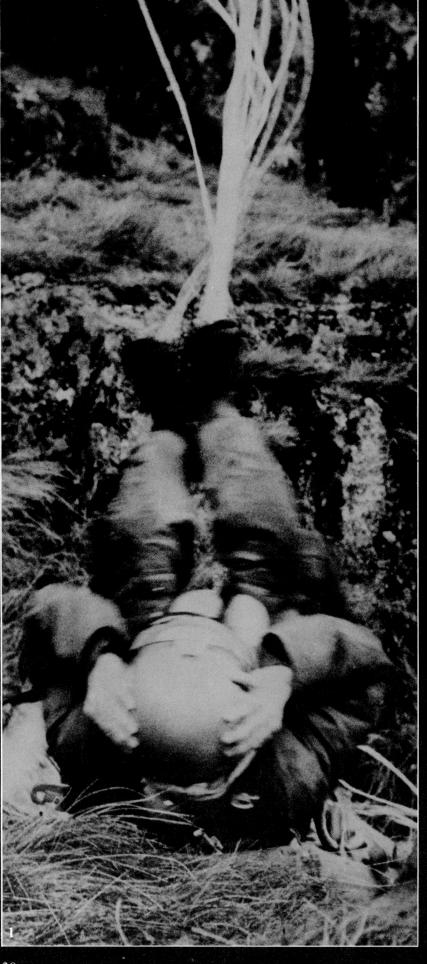

A Leap into the Unknown

John says: I like parachuting—but I like to be the one who decides when to jump.

For thousands of years, sailors have dreaded the words "Abandon ship", and ever since aeroplanes were invented pilots have lived with the idea that one day things might go so wrong that their only hope would be a leap into the unknown at the end of a parachute.

What is it like to be a stranded, injured pilot, alone on a bare mountain?

What is it like to be a member of the RAF Mountain Rescue team called out to search for a solitary figure among the rocks in the middle of winter?

To answer the first question, I volunteered to play the part of a missing pilot with a broken leg, stranded 400 feet from the ground on a mountainside in Wales.

The team had no idea where I was, and they had the additional lumber of a new recruit—Master Mountaineer Purves.

This was the first time I'd had a go at mountaineering, and strictly between you and me, I wasn't really looking forward to it.

Some people, like Johnny, have absolutely no fear of heights. I wouldn't say I was terrified, but–we'll put it this way–if they want a chap to stay on the ground, I wouldn't mind volunteering. But today they didn't want a man to stay on the ground. We were going to make the initial climb in two 2-man teams, attacking the mountain in different directions so that a thorough search for the missing pilot could be made. I was to climb with Chris Dumbill, who's been a member of the team for five years, so at least I had the comfort of being in experienced hands.

It was bitterly cold, with an icy drizzle in the wind, when we started to sort out our gear at the foot of the mountain.

Chris showed me how to tie a mountaineer's knot, called a tarbuck, which makes a loop at the end of the rope that clips into a special fixing on the front part of the belt. Chris tied another tarbuck on his end of the rope, and, securely bound together, we began to make our ascent.

Only one man climbs at a time in a two-man team, the other man makes a belay of rope round his waist so that, if the climber falls, his mate should be able to stop him from crashing to his death in the valley below.

Just as he started to climb, Chris looked over his shoulder:

"I'd wear gloves if I were you, Pete. If I should fall, that rope will burn the skin off your hands in no time."

With that comforting thought, I clung onto the end of the rope and watched Chris climb slowly and carefully up the face.

Far away to the right I could see the other pair of climbers looking like flies as they scrambled round a great over-hanging rock. Any moment now it was going to be my turn.

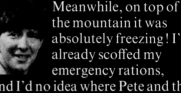 Meanwhile, on top of the mountain it was absolutely freezing! I'd already scoffed my emergency rations, and I'd no idea where Pete and the others were. If they didn't rescue me soon, they'd have a real casualty on their hands–suffering from frostbite and exposure!

 Chris Dumbill put on his gloves, wrapped the rope round his waist, and looked down through his boots at me–20 feet below.

1 & 2 John played the part of a pilot who had baled out and landed on top of a mountain with a broken leg.
3 Peter joined the RAF Mountain Rescue team on an exercise to find John.
4 Chris showed him how to tie a mountaineer's knot called a tarbuck.
5 Roped together Chris and Peter began to climb the mountain.

31

"OK Pete. Watch it round that jagged rock—you may find it a bit slippery."

"Right, Chris. Climbing now." This was it.

I'd made a careful note of every foot and handhold that Chris had taken.

I was just beginning to feel slightly less terrified when it started—just a few feathery flakes at first, then the wind built up from a whistle to a howl, and in a matter of seconds, we were in the middle of a raging blizzard. All the time I'd been trying not to look down at the distant valley, but now I didn't have to worry, it had entirely disappeared in a mass of swirling snow!

Above me, Chris was non-chalantly taking in the rope as I inched my way up the mountain.

"Do you often have to turn out in weather like this?" I gasped.

"All the time," he said, grinning down at me. "Funny thing—no one ever seems to need rescuing on a nice, bright, sunny day."

"I've only got one foothold here," I said with a forced calmness.

Suddenly, I was in a panic. My hands were bent numb with cold,

I was half-blinded by snow, and Chris was still a clear 10 feet above me.

"Round to your left, Pete—no, that's too far—now a bit higher. That's it!"

To my everlasting relief, I felt my boot crunch home into a crevice in the rock—and I started breathing again.

We scrambled up the last few feet of the mountain together—and there, huddled in his parachute, and covered in biscuit crumbs, was a cold but cheerful John Noakes.

But that didn't mean our troubles were over. John was supposed to have broken his leg, and a man with a broken leg can't move. Somehow we had to get him down to the ambulance, and between us and the ambulance was 400 feet of sheer rock face.

"Don't worry, Johnny, there's a stretcher on its way up," said Chris Dumbill.

"Are they bringing a hot-water bottle, too?" asked John.

"If there is one, I'm having it," I said, blowing on my freezing fingers.

The stretcher party, headed by team leader Pat McGowan, ap-

Slowly, inch by inch, I clambered over the rocks until, with snow swirling in my face, I came to the ledge where Chris was waiting for me.

peared out of the blizzard, looking like men from Scott's last expedition. Chris Dumbill had already examined John's leg, diagnosed a fracture of the femur and put him in splints. All the mountain rescue team are fully qualified first-aiders. Next, John was zipped into an enormous padded bag, strapped onto a stretcher and, looking like something out of Pharaoh's tomb, was carried to the edge of the mountain.

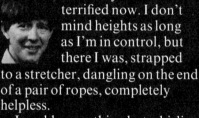

It was my turn to feel terrified now. I don't mind heights as long as I'm in control, but there I was, strapped to a stretcher, dangling on the end of a pair of ropes, completely helpless.

I could see nothing but whirling snow and a black sky above me, but behind my back I knew that there was 400 feet of nothing.

Pat McGowan and Dave Robinson were walking backwards down the cliff, gently guiding the stretcher in front of them.

They were being lowered on one rope, and I was on the other. Pat was in radio communication with the men at the top, so he could give instructions all the way down.

"Lower rope 1 – Easy now –"

They walked slowly backwards down the mountain until their heads were just above me.

"Right, now 1 and 2 together – slowly."

This time we all went down together, the boys guiding the stretcher with their hands, and pushing away from the mountain with their feet.

Gradually, inch by inch, we

made our way over the icy rocks until at last, with scarcely a bump, the stretcher came to rest at the foot of the mountain.

It was over.

The RAF Mountain Rescue team had completed another successful operation.

At the top of the mountain lay Noakes swathed in his parachute. We strapped him firmly to the stretcher, and carried him to the edge of the precipice. Then with Pat and Dave walking backwards down the mountain, we gently lowered him to the ground.

Explorer's Kit

Mountaineering and arctic exploring need special equipment. Here are some ideas for things to make for your soldier doll to help him survive an arctic winter. There's a sledge, an ice-axe, snow goggles, and a climbing rope – and all of them can be made from scraps.

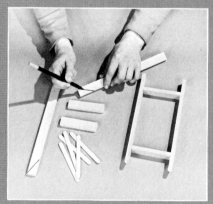

1 The Sledge For the frame you will need two lengths of wood about 10 inches long and ½ an inch wide, and two more pieces a bit shorter than a lolly stick. The two long pieces are the runners, so saw off the front ends to make them slope. Sand-paper all the wood smooth.

2 Fix the runners apart with the two smaller pieces of wood. You can stick them with impact adhesive, or you could use panel-pins for a really strong job. The slats on the sledge are lolly sticks or balsa strip. You will need about 13 slats and it's a good idea to mark their positions on the frame before sticking them in place.

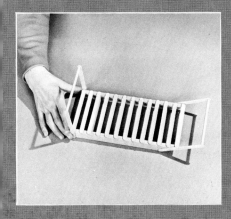 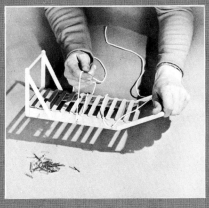 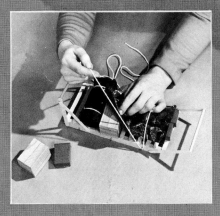

3 Both ends of the sledge are made in the same way. Cut a piece of ¼-inch dowel the same length as a lolly stick. Glue or panel-pin a stick to each end of the dowel. Glue the front end along the slope of the runners and the back end upright.

4 For extra strength for the back upright, stick two more lolly sticks from the top sloping down to the runners. Then knock two or three panel-pins halfway into the side of the runners and bend them down into hooks. These are to hold the rope.

5 Rope the supplies in place with a piece of white string. Paint matchboxes to take your explorer's supplies, make bedding rolls from scraps of materials, and cover all the equipment with a small piece of plastic to keep it snow-proof.

6 The Equipment The climbing rope is a coil of white string. Cut the shape of the axe from a plastic bottle and cover it with silver paper. Make a tiny hole in the axe and push it down onto the handle, which is a manicure stick. To make the goggles, cut two rings from the top part of a plastic soap bottle where the soap comes out. Fix them together with fuse wire and tie on some thin elastic to go round your explorer's head. Glue the goggles firmly onto a piece of coloured cellophane. When the glue is dry, cut away the spare cellophane.

"A very queer small boy"
The Childhood of Charles Dickens

1 Gad's Hill Place–the great mansion Charles Dickens admired when he was a small boy and bought when he became rich and famous.

2 When Dickens was only 12 years old, his father was sent to the Marshalsea Prison for being in debt. Charles went to visit him every week.

On New Year's Day, 1970, we told the story of Charles Dickens, who died exactly a hundred years ago, and whose books and stories are still read all over the world.

Soon afterwards, we were fascinated to have a letter from Blue Peter viewer *Susan Debnam*, telling us that she actually goes to school at Gad's Hill Place, the very house that Charles Dickens bought when he was rich and famous.

By then he was so well known, he not only lived in a grand 19-roomed mansion, but he even had a tunnel built from the grounds of his house, so that he could leave without being recognised. But when he was a little boy, no-one would have imagined that Charles Dickens was destined to become a great man.

He was born in 1812, in a little house in Portsmouth. His father, John Dickens, who was a poor clerk in the Navy Pay Office, was dreadfully muddle-headed about money, but he was very kind and cheerful, and always hoping that something would turn up to set the family on its feet.

Charles' mother, Elizabeth, was a foolish, fussy creature, longing for a fashionable life. She never learned to cope with the problems of her growing, hard-up family.

Then John Dickens was moved to Chatham, and the family lived in a little house in the town. It was not very grand, but nearby was Rochester, a lovely city with a cathedral and a castle and boats on its wide, beautiful river.

3 The blacking factory where Dickens was sent to work as a boy, sticking labels on bottles.

Little Charles was now five years old, and he loved Rochester, and the pleasant life the family led. At school, he learned to read, and he became intrigued by stories of adventure and travel. And then he began to make up stories for himself.

He went for long walks with his father through the countryside, and saw the stage coaches on their way to London. Quite often they passed a great house which Charles admired very much–it was called Gad's Hill. He was so fond of it, his father used to say jokingly, "You might some day come to live in it yourself."

All his life, Charles remembered those happy

years, and remembered what he was like himself—"a very queer small boy"—but he was never to be so happy again.

Bad times came, and once more the family had to move. This time, though, they went to London, and dark days set in for them all. They lived miserably in a wretched dingy street, as John Dickens began to get more deeply into debt. He could not even afford to send nine-year-old Charles to school, so the boy just roamed the streets of London day after day.

His family needed money so desperately that a job was found for Charles, and he was sent to work. He was paid six shillings a week for sticking labels on bottles, in a filthy blacking warehouse down by the river.

And then John Dickens was arrested and put into prison, because he could not pay back the money he had borrowed. He was sent to the Marshalsea Prison, but although he had to stay inside, it was fairly comfortable, and his wife and younger children were allowed to stay in the prison with him.

But not Charles! He had to stay at his job, and now he had to find lodgings and buy food out of his six shillings a week. He was miserably lonely, and hungry and neglected and ill. He felt desperate. He was utterly without hope—"No words can express the secret agony of my soul," he wrote later. And

Charles Dickens never forgot his own despair, or the wretchedness of the stunted lives of the other children of the London streets.

Then, quite unexpectedly, the nightmare came to an end.

John Dickens inherited some money so he was able to pay his debts. He was let out of prison, and the first thing he did was to go straight to the blacking warehouse and take Charles home.

But Mrs Dickens was horrified—the wages Charles earned were very useful, so she insisted that he should go back to work, and Charles remembered this years later when his mother was an old lady. "I never afterwards forgot, I never can forget, that my mother was warm for my being sent back." But his father refused, and although Charles went to school again, sometimes he sat apart, wondering what the other boys would say, if they knew about those dreadful months in the blacking factory.

Soon he was fifteen and left school for ever. He became a clerk in a lawyer's office and in his spare time he haunted the library of the British Museum, and in its crowded Reading Room he began a new study—Shorthand! It was a new invention then, and was used for taking down speeches. Charles went to the House of Commons for all the most important debates. He sat in the gallery with the other reporters, writing down the speeches to appear next morning in the newspapers. He became known as the fastest reporter in Parliament.

Before long, Charles Dickens was the top journalist of a London newspaper called the *Morning Chronicle*. He led a busy life, hurrying by coach all over the country to cover important stories, trying to be first with the news. But he wanted instant fame! He brooded on his chances, as he wrote stories on his own account, tearing up manuscript after manuscript.

Then, one day, he risked it! He posted a story to the Editor of a magazine. It was accepted, and he was asked to write more. In the month that he was 24, these stories were published together as a book.

Now he was an author—and his first two novels—*Pickwick Papers* and *Oliver Twist*—had an enormous success.

At 30, Charles Dickens, rich and famous, was the most popular novelist of the day. At last he had escaped from the blacking factory and the slum streets!

He bought Gad's Hill, the house that "very queer small boy" had admired so much and he wrote book after book, for years, about all the peculiar people he had met in his strange, crowded life.

But as he looked back over his busy life as it drew towards its end, he felt, he said, that there was "something wanting—always something wanting", for that small boy had lost love and trust and happiness, and Charles Dickens never really found them again.

4 Charles Dickens, aged 30, writing at Gad's Hill when he was a famous author.

Blue Peter Spectacular

Every so often, we have a great scoop on Blue Peter, and this happened a few months ago when the famous Red Army Dance Ensemble from Russia managed to fit in a visit to the Blue Peter studio, in the middle of their crowded tour of the British Isles.

It all began when Mrs Victor Hockhauser, the wife of the well-known Impresario, telephoned our office.

"You can have them at 9.30 on Monday morning. They'll be travelling from Bournemouth on Sunday night – and they must be at Wimbledon at 1.30 sharp for important rehearsals. Will you have enough time ?"

Yes we would ! Thanks to video tape recording, the short time the Russians could spend with us was no problem. They could rehearse and record their dances in the morning all ready for our programme at five to five that afternoon.

But entertaining a foreign touring company is quite tricky.

There were 12 dancers and two musicians and not one of them spoke a word of English. Imagine trying to mime instructions like "When the Floor Manager gives a signal, dance down stage until you reach the mark on the floor. Then do the cartwheels and the back somersaults !" They wouldn't have reached Wimbledon by midnight, let alone 1.30 p.m., unless we'd had some help. Fortunately, we knew of an excellent interpreter – Mrs

Barr – who spoke perfect Russian and would be able to explain exactly what we wanted the dancers to do.

Then there were notices to prepare: **ТУАЛЕТ МУЖСКОЙ** which is Russian for ''Gentlemen'', to pin on the lavatory door; several **АРТИСТИЧЕСКАЯ УБОРНАЯ** for the dressing rooms, and **СТУДИЯ** for our studio.

We telephoned the Canteen Manageress:

''Blue Peter speaking – please can you organise lunch for 14 Russians at 12.15 on Monday?''

The Manageress could, and she suggested that to save time a choice of three main dishes – ravioli, fried fish and roast chicken – would be available. She also promised to see the dancers didn't have to spend too long queueing up in the canteen.

On the dot of 9.30 a.m., the Russians' coach parked outside the studio, and the dancers walked into the entrance hall looking for all the world like a group of city businessmen in their dark suits and overcoats.

By the time they reached the Blue Peter studio, they'd changed into their uniforms – but they still didn't look much like dancers.

We'd all been practising a few words of Russian like **СПАСИБО** (Thank you) and **ЗДРАВСТВУЙТЕ** (Hello) and **ДОСВИДАНИЯ** (Goodbye), so we thought now was the time to try them out. John said **СПАСИБО** by mistake, but the Russians thought it was a huge joke and grinned a lot. The ice was broken.

Mrs Barr introduced us all, and we exchanged autographs, and the dancers drank orange squash from plastic BBC cups which they seemed to think were very smart.

Then the rehearsals began in earnest. The three of us watched in amazement as the Russians charged around the studio – leaping and bounding at breakneck speed. Alexander, the leading dancer, had shown me a few of his steps earlier on, and I'd tried some of them out. But I couldn't even do one of the jumps without falling over – let alone 25 of them non-stop!

All the dancers did their own special solo pieces, each one a series of spectacular movements. Alexander's consisted of

9.30 a.m. As the Russians arrived, I pinned up a vital notice. With not one of the dancers speaking a word of English, everything had to be translated.

9.45 a.m. The dancers had changed into their uniforms and were ready to rehearse. We all exchanged autographs after we'd been introduced.

10.00 a.m. Mrs Barr, our Interpreter, explained exactly what we wanted the Russians to do. Each movement had to be carefully worked out.

Alexander made the steps look so easy I thought I'd have a go. After all, I'd spent a very tough day at the Royal Ballet School in Richmond Park, so Russian dancing seemed a piece of cake.

So far so good – even if I did look a bit clumsy. But now I was beginning to feel a little less confident. My legs just wouldn't go in the right directions – I couldn't do the step slowly, let alone at Alexander's break-neck speed!

Total defeat! This was the moment that Noakes decided to leave Russian dancing to the Russians.

the most fantastic jumps we'd ever seen. He did the splits in mid-air – whilst he was leaping higher than our "Blue Peter" shelves!

By the time the Russians were ready to record, the atmosphere in the studio was electric. The two accordionists played tunes that would have set a statue dancing. We were all tapping our feet and so were the engineers and the scenemen and the electricians. When the recording was over, there was a burst of spontaneous applause from all over the studio – something you very rarely hear unless a performance is absolutely exceptional.

We all relaxed to wait for the "clear". After a Video Tape recording, the engineers

always have to play the recording back to check there are no technical faults. At the same time it can be seen on the studio monitor – so the dancers crowded round the television set to watch. It seemed to us that it was the first time they'd ever seen themselves in action – and judging by their smiles, they obviously enjoyed every moment of their performance.

There was a thumbs-up sign from Derek, our Floor Manager – we were clear – the recording was perfect. But it was such a treat for the dancers, we had it played back again.

Val gave Alexander a "Blue Peter" badge, and there was more autograph swopping. In spite of the language barrier, we could have gone on for

hours – until Mrs Barr reminded us of the time.

By 12.15, the Russians were at the counter of the BBC's canteen. We noticed they were all having a pretty hefty lunch –"No wonder after all that leaping about," Val said. But even Val was surprised to see what was actually on their laden plates. Instead of choosing *between* the ravioli, fried fish and roast chicken, they'd all had the lot – and all of it sloshed onto one plate! And one particularly hungry dancer had taken all the supplies of rolls and butter for the whole canteen.

Like the playback, lunch was a great success – and our morning with the Red Army Dance Ensemble was one we would certainly not forget in a hurry!

10.30 a.m. Now the rehearsal had really started. We watched in amazement as the Russians began their clapping and shouting – as the dances became faster, the shouting grew louder.

Some of the steps were extraordinarily difficult. You have to be very fit indeed to dance very fast in a squatting position.

12.00 The dancers crowded round the studio monitor to watch their performance being played back. It seemed to be the first time they'd ever seen themselves in action on a television screen.

12.10 p.m. We thought Alexander really deserved his Blue Peter badge. After all that leaping and shouting, he didn't seem the slightest bit exhausted.

12.15 p.m. The Russians joined us for lunch in the BBC Canteen. They had ravioli, fried fish and roast chicken, and one dancer took all the supplies of rolls and butter for the whole canteen!

Do you know what Stilt fishing is?
We found out when we went to Ceylon.

When the south-west monsoon blows and whips up the seas into great roaring breakers, the fishermen on the extreme south coast of Ceylon can't put out in their small, outrigger fishing boats.

Instead, they go for the shallow-water fish called Korrumburua which are used in the hottest curries. The fish are easily frightened, but hundreds of years ago, south-coast fishermen found a unique way of catching the shy, quicksilver Korrumburua that has carried on to this day.

They perch, rod in hand, on slender wooden poles, topped with a crossbar that's just big enough for a man to sit on.

We suddenly came across them as we drove along the south coast. Thirty almost naked, motionless men sitting in a row like storks, with their rods extended over the boiling surf. It's a tough life, sitting on a small narrow branch all day, under the baking sun. John and Peter tried it for one hour and complained of sore bottoms for a week!

BLEEP and BOOSTER

Bleep and Booster's holiday had come to an end. For a whole week they'd been camping on the shores of Stellarus Lake, and that night they were due back in Miron City. It had been a funny sort of holiday, for like all Mirons, Bleep was happy in any atmosphere –gas, air or water, it was all the same to him! At this moment he was sitting on a rock at the very bottom of the lake, having his lunch, whilst all around him strange fishes swam in and out of weird sea plants.

"Poor old Booster," thought Bleep as he swallowed the last drop from his Asteroidade bottle and gave the remaining crumb from his stellar paste sandwiches to a passing Galaxy fish. "I think he's had quite a good time sitting on the shore inventing things, but it can't be as much fun as this. I know what, I'll take him a present." So he grabbed some passing Stellarus shrimps, popped them in the empty asteroidade bottle with a few little weeds to keep them happy, and began the long swim to the surface.

Meanwhile, Booster had packed all their gear back in the space pod ready for take-off, and he, too, had had a marvellous day.

"I've really done it this time!" he thought. "My latest invention is my greatest!" He was almost bursting with excitement as he waited for Bleep to come back, so to pass the time he took out his pocket-knife and started to carve a boat from a piece of the wood-like weed that grew along the shore.

"I'll give it to Bleep," he thought. "Then I'll show him my invention," and his eyes filled with pride as he looked at the black metal box with the glowing lens that lay on the shore beside him.

An hour later, Bleep broke surface and the two boys ran to meet each other. They were delighted with their presents. There was nothing in space like the little wooden yacht with its paper sails and string rigging. It was the best toy that Bleep had ever had, and Booster was equally delighted by the curiously spiked Stellarus shrimps and the weird frond-like weeds.

"There's nothing on Earth like them," he said, "and there's nothing like this, either." He picked up his latest invention and gave it to Bleep.

"What is it?" asked Bleep, suspiciously.

"It's my Expanda Ray box. Go on! Try it! Point it at the ship and press the button!"

Bleep felt a bit doubtful. He'd been caught by Booster's inventions before, but it seemed rude to refuse, so he shut his eyes and did what he was told.

There was a blinding flash and Bleep opened his eyes. Where his little boat had been stood an enormous great ship.

"It's my Expanda Ray that did it," cried Booster excitedly. "It makes everything at least twenty times bigger. Don't you think it's clever?" But instead of being delighted, Bleep was quite annoyed.

"It's idiotic," he said. "How can I get my ship back to Miron? It'll never fit in the space pod."

Booster had never thought of that, but he wasn't going to say so. Disappointment and anger swept over him and he shouted crossly:

"I've given you an enormous present and you ought to be grateful. All you've given me is a measly old bottle of shrimps!" And he grabbed the Expanda Ray box from Bleep, aimed at the bottle, and fired.

Instantly, the bottle cracked open and crawling and slithering towards them came the Stellarus shrimps, not tiny now, but huge monsters with menacing spikes and claws.

For a second, Bleep and Booster froze with horror. Then Bleep saw that the little fronds of weed had grown into tough, leathery tentacles that were slowly inching along the shore and beginning to envelop their feet.

"The ray guns," he shouted. "Where are they?"

"I've packed them," cried Booster. "They're in the space pod. Quick, run for it!"

They ran up the beach and flung themselves breathlessly inside. Booster threw the Expanda Ray box in a corner and grabbed a ray gun.

"I'll fend them off, Bleep, while you ignite the rocket motors," he cried. "It's only two minutes to ignition, so we're bound to get away."

But Booster had spoken too soon. Though he'd switched to double destructor power, the ray gun had no effect on the advancing monsters. Already their claws were beginning to scrabble on the surface of the machine, and Booster had time only to kick away a leathery tentacle that had crept inside and slam the hatch door shut before the huge monsters were crawling all over the space pod.

"Just in time," cried Bleep as the door clanged shut. "Stand by for take-off. 3, 2, 1, zero . . . We have lift-off!"

The rocket motors roared and the boys braced themselves thankfully for take-off. They were saved! But seconds later they looked at the controls in horror. Though the rockets had ignited, they were only an inch or two off the ground!

"We're trapped!" cried Booster. "The weight of the monsters on the roof is holding us down. The rocket motors aren't powerful enough. They're using their claws like tin-openers and they'll be on

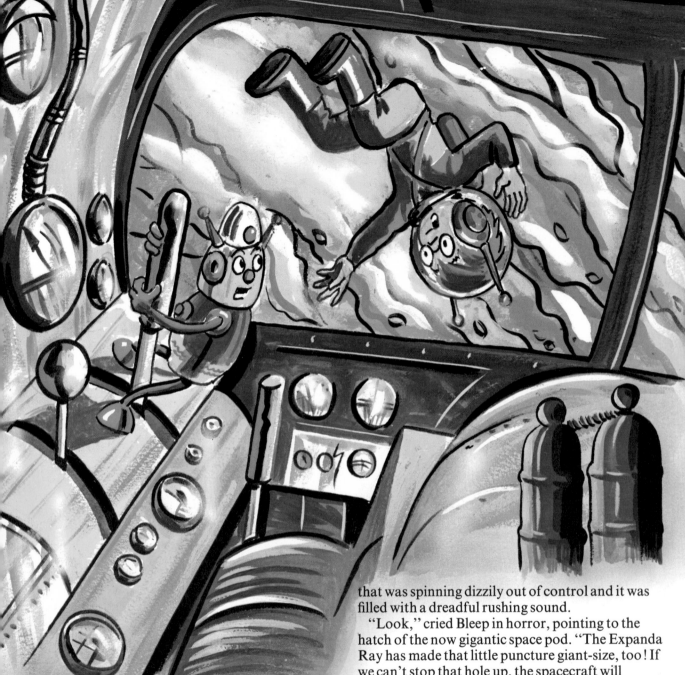

us any minute! They've already punctured the hatch! Oh, Bleep, what can we do?"

Bleep looked at the tiny hole and thought quickly.

"I know," he yelled, "we'll use your invention. If it can turn shrimps into monsters, it can turn a space pod into a space freighter," and he grabbed the Expanda Ray box from the floor and began to fire all round the cabin.

The little cabin filled with a blinding light and the noise of the rocket motors became deafening as, with tremendous force, the boys felt themselves shooting through space.

For a moment they lost consciousness, but when they came round they found themselves clinging to the bulkheads of an enormous spacecraft, far bigger even than Space Freighter 9—but it was a spacecraft

that was spinning dizzily out of control and it was filled with a dreadful rushing sound.

"Look," cried Bleep in horror, pointing to the hatch of the now gigantic space pod. "The Expanda Ray has made that little puncture giant-size, too! If we can't stop that hole up, the spacecraft will crumple like a paper bag. Think, Booster! Think of something to save us!"

Booster thought for a second. Then from his pocket he brought a little packet of Gamma Gum-drops which were his favourite sweets. He put three of them in his mouth and started chewing frantically.

"Booster," cried Bleep desperately. "Don't eat sweets—think of something!" But Booster went on chewing and chewing. Then suddenly he spat out the Gamma Gumdrops, aimed the Expanda Ray box at them and fired. There, on the floor, was a huge sticky mass, and without wasting a moment, Booster grabbed it in handfuls and packed it into the hole.

"It'll set like a jelly," he said. "It'll hold until we get to Miron City. Check the controls and see where we are."

Bleep climbed up on the giant pilot's seat and looked at the Scanner Screens. Now that the hole

was filled up, the craft had stopped spinning, but as he plotted a course for Miron, an awful thought struck him. The control levers were now so huge that he hadn't the strength to move them!

Quickly he checked his navigation charts. The course they were on was taking them straight to Furnaceous, the hottest planet in the Galaxy–and unless they changed course within seconds, their space ship would be burnt to a cinder.

"Quick, Booster!" he cried, as he struggled with the retro-rocket lever, "help me! We must change course or die!"

Already the cabin was getting hotter, but however hard the boys strained, they couldn't shift the lever even a millimetre. Now on the Video Screen they could see the white-hot flames shooting from Furnaceous. The next moment red-hot fireballs whizzed past the observation window as Bleep and Booster clung together helplessly. Any minute now a fireball would strike them, and both of them knew that there would be no escape! They said goodbye, held hands and waited.

CRASH! The explosion when it came was tremendous. Everything broke loose and hurtled round the cabin. Bleep, hanging on desperately with his suction feet, saw Booster flung past upside down and heard him smash into the wall.

Then there was silence. As the seconds passed the cabin grew cooler. Bleep, amazed, found he was still alive. What miracle had saved him? His first thoughts were for Booster, and when he spotted him, he couldn't help laughing. He was stuck head first in the Gamma Gumdrop patch! The sticky jelly had broken his fall and he wasn't hurt at all. Bleep helped him struggle free, and then seeing that in spite of everything the Video Screen was still working, they rushed to find out where they were and what had happened. When they saw the screen, they could hardly believe their eyes. Bright and clear they could see the planet Miron–and Miracle of Miracles, they were safely in orbit round it!

"The fireball must have ignited our spare rocket fuel tank," said Booster. "The blast from the explosion has acted like a rocket boost and we've been blasted into a safety orbit."

"And we're in range for my transmitter," cried Bleep. "Now we can get help!" and immediately he called up Miron Space Centre.

"Bleep, Bleep. Emergency. Bleep and Booster calling. We are in orbit round Miron. Our ship is out of action. Please rescue us."

At once came the welcome voice of the Space Centre Controller promising help within an hour.

The boys settled down happily to wait and Booster picked up his Expanda Ray box. It was undamaged.

"Don't!" said Bleep. "Please don't fire it again. It's brought us nothing but trouble."

"Just once more," said Booster, "and then I'll destroy it," and he took from his pocket a rather small Star Fruit. Flash! Bleep laughed as he saw the enormous orange-coloured fruit.

"Perhaps your Expanda Ray's not such a bad invention after all, Booster," he said, and they both settled down happily with a large, juicy slice, to wait for the lights of the Miron Emergency Rescue Craft.

Celebration Cakes

Have you ever wanted a cake to celebrate a special occasion? Or for a particularly important tea party? This rose-decorated straw hat could be the answer! It's covered in a thick layer of creamy butter icing – I've flavoured mine with chocolate – but you can make yours any colour or flavour you like. Your friends will never guess that the "hat" started off as an ordinary 2/6d. sponge (or you could even bake the sponge base yourself if you had plenty of time) and the coloured roses give the cake a really professional look, like something produced at that smart hotel where John once learned how to be a waiter. But they're so simple that anyone could make them – even someone who's usually not at all good at cooking.

And if you don't want to make the straw hat, you can transform small cup cakes by decorating them with single roses – just like the one I'm eating in the picture.

But before you make the roses you'll need to ice your cake, and this is what you do:

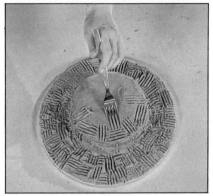

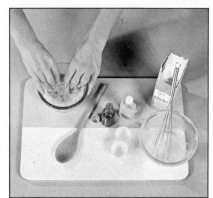

1 Butter Icing This is just *4 oz. of margarine* and *8 oz. of icing sugar* mixed together. Beat until the mixture turns almost white in colour – your wrists will ache! To make chocolate icing add *2 dessertspoonsful of chocolate powder* (or 2 oz. of melted chocolate). Add coffee powder if you prefer a coffee-flavoured cake, and by using a few drops of colouring you can turn the icing pink or green.

Put your sponge on a cake board or large plate – this will be the brim of the hat. And with a spatula or big knife, spread the icing all over the cake and the board, or plate.

2 Cover the cake and the board with a pattern made by using a fork. You can see how the finished effect looks like woven straw. When your fork gets clogged with the butter icing, wipe it clean and dip it into a bowl of hot water before starting on the next bit of the pattern. You will find you will probably have to do this quite often. You can also keep your spatula clean in the same way when icing the cake. This will give the cake a really smooth surface before you start on the pattern.

3 The Rose Mixture You can make the roses from marzipan, or the sort of mixture you use for peppermint creams – without the peppermint. This mixture is far cheaper than marzipan, and you will need: *1 lb. of icing sugar; one lightly whisked egg white; ½ teaspoonful of glycerine* and some *colouring*.

Mix the white of egg and the icing sugar together. Start off with a spoon and finish with your hands. Add a few drops of colouring, and also the glycerine. The glycerine is not essential, but it will stop the mixture becoming too dry.

4 Making the Roses Mould a small piece of the mixture into a triangle shape with a rounded point. The tip of the point will be the centre of your rose. Roll five smaller pieces into small balls and squash each one flat. These are the five petals. Wrap one petal round the top of the triangle, then add the others, attaching the centre of each new petal to the join of the one already on the triangle.

5 When all the petals are wrapped round the top of the triangle, cut them off with a sharp knife. (The part of the triangle that is left behind can be built up to form the foundation for your next rose.) Gently bend the tips of some of the petals to get the effect you want. You can vary the size of your roses to suit the size of your cake, and you can make rose buds, too.

6 Decorating the Hat Make as many roses as you want to put round the brim of the hat and save two or three of the best ones for the top.

I made the leaves by colouring some butter icing green and placing it on the cake with the tip of a sharp-pointed knife.

Don't worry if you spoil a few roses to start with, you can just put them back in the bowl and remould them.

"You go in for the close-ups, John"

"That's what BBC's Ace Newscameraman Bill Baglin said to me when we went to cover a bank raid story together."

"You never know what's going to happen when you walk into the office in the morning," said Bill as we sat in the News Cameramen's Rest Room at the Television Centre. "You might be on a plane for America in half an hour – or else trying to look inconspicuous at the Lord Mayor's banquet, or maybe hanging out of a helicopter hovering over a North Sea Oil Rig in a force 5 gale. Then there are days like today when Blue Peter comes to see how busy you are, and nothing happens at all. Have a cup of coffee?"

I was just raising the coffee to my lips when the radio on the desk crackled, and a voice said:

"Bill Baglin there, please?"

Bill leant over and pressed down a key.

"Speak," he said to the radio.

"Oh Bill," said the voice. "We've got a bank raid in Dulwich Village. I'll give you more gen on the radio if you'll get on the way."

"Bank raid – Dulwich Village," repeated Bill. "O.K., we're off."

Two minutes later we were roaring out of the Television Centre in a car packed with loaded cameras, and driven by Bill's Sound Recordist, Eric Thirer.

As we weaved in and out of the London traffic bound for Dulwich Village, the radio crackled again, this time it was the two-way car radio. Newsmen are rarely far away from the voice of Spur Base at the Television Centre.

"Spur Base to Aerial 9."

On Bill's instructions, I picked up the microphone.

"Aerial 9. Go ahead."

1 On the Intercom the Film Operations Chief told Bill and John that a bank raid story had just broken in Dulwich. 2 Seconds later they were roaring out of the TV Centre in a fast camera car. 3 As they drove the Centre radioed the exact address of the bank. 4 Bill gave me the second camera and pointed to a policeman across the road.

"Further information on the bank raid," crackled the voice. "Address : 117 Dulwich Village. Still not sure how much money has been stolen. A reporter will meet you on location. Two men coshed. Bandits escaped in a gold-coloured Cortina. Despatch rider will meet you to collect your first film – over."

I glanced at Bill who nodded from the back of the car.

"Aerial 9 to Spur Base," I said into the microphone. "Over and listening."

Soon the car screeched to a halt outside 117 Dulwich Village. I'd expected the place to be surrounded by police and reporters, but apart from the fact that the bank door was closed and there was a policeman outside, it could have been any ordinary Tuesday morning.

Bill and Eric leapt out of the car and grabbed their equipment from the boot. Bill stuck the second camera in my hand –

"There's a policeman doing a house-to-house enquiry across the road. Let's go over and get some shots of him."

I hadn't actually noticed the policeman, but Bill's experienced eye had taken in the whole scene the moment we arrived, so I obediently followed him across the road.

He watched the policeman for a second, checked that both

cameras had the correct exposure, and then turned to me and said :

"John, when the policeman walks up the path to the next house, you follow him right up to the door and get some close shots."

I must admit I wasn't all that keen on walking up close behind the policeman, but I didn't want to refuse my first assignment, so I shouldered my camera, switched on, and marched boldly up the path, keeping the bobbing helmet firmly in the centre of my viewfinder.

The policeman rang the doorbell, and I eased back to make a two-shot, as the woman

answered the door.

Then the helmet turned towards me and a voice said quietly, but firmly,

"Shove off, mate !"

I gave a sheepish grin and scuttled off to find Bill who'd been shooting a general view from the gate.

"Well done, John," he smiled. "Let's go to the bank now, shall we ?"

The reporter was waiting for us outside the bank. He'd already made contact with the Bank Manager and arranged to do an interview. Eric, the Sound Recordist, was standing by, ear-phones on his head, and a gun-mike, which looks like an enormous sausage, held in his right hand.

Bill squinted into his viewfinder.

"Right, John, I'll cover it from here with the Sound Camera. You go in tight and get some nice close shots."

"O.K. Camera running."

Before I knew where I was, the Bank Manager had arrived and the reporter was saying to him :

"What actually happened at the bank this morning ?"

The moment the interview was over, we whipped the film out of the cameras, "canned it up'', and stuck it into the saddle bag of the despatch rider's throbbing motor-cycle.

He picked up a microphone that was clipped to his petrol tank and said:

''Aerial 5 to Spur Base. Over.''

''Aerial 5 go ahead,'' came back a familiar voice.

''Have collected film from Bill Baglin and John Noakes at Dulwich Village – and I'm on my way back.''

His engine roared and he disappeared in a cloud of exhaust fumes, leaving Bill and me to pack up and return to the Television Centre.

The bulletin was due on the air in an hour's time, and the film was still undeveloped, unseen, unedited and unwritten.

Within seconds of arrival, it was pushed into the developing bath, dried off, and then projected onto two screens in different parts of the building, one watched by sub-Editor Alan Kumm who writes the story, the other by Film Editor Martin O'Collins who cuts the film to Alan's instructions.

Martin's 'phone rang as soon

5-9 On Bill's instruction, I switched on the camera and followed the policeman up the drive. As we reached the door he turned to me and said ''Shove off, mate''. Seconds later I was outside the bank with Bill, shooting an interview with the Bank Manager, then I rushed the film to the waiting despatch rider.

5

6

7

8

9

10

11

12

13

14

15

16

10 & 11 "I'm on my way," he said into his microphone and roared off. 12 Half an hour later, at the TV Centre, Martin, the Film Editor, began cutting the film, 13 and Alan, the Sub-Editor, checked the order of shots on the phone before writing the script. 14 The Director warned 15 Richard Baker to stand by for a late story. 16 "30 seconds to go," shouted the Studio Manager.

as the film had been shown.

"Alan here. Start with a general view of the bank – ten seconds of the house–to–house search – and then straight into the interview."

As Martin started to cut the film, Alan rolled a sheet of paper into his typewriter and wrote:

Bank Raid.

This morning a Bank Manager was injured when a shot was fired . . .

In the control room, the Studio Director picks up the 'phone and speaks to Newsreader Richard Baker:

"Hello Dickie. We have a late story – New lead. Bank raid. Just coming in !"

"Thirty seconds to go, studio," shouts the Floor Manager.

The staccato notes of the News signature tune roared out on the air, and I proudly watched *my* shot of the bank appear on the screen. Richard Baker cleared his throat and said:

"This morning a Bank Manager was injured when a shot was fired . . ."

Wild Cats

1,100 miles away from Britain, one of the world's largest colonies of wild cats lives in the heart of a great city – Italy's capital, Rome.

Nearly 2,000 years ago, the Forum was the fashionable centre of the city. The streets and pavements were crowded with Roman soldiers in scarlet cloaks and citizens in their long, flowing, white togas. But the Forum was pulled to pieces when the barbarian hordes overran the city. Today there are crumbling ruins where the great colonnades once stood. And the very spot where once Roman citizens went about their business has been taken over by prowling wild cats.

Some of them started life as ordinary domestic cats – but were lost or abandoned and found their way to the ruins. It's not a bad place to live if you're a cat with nowhere else to go. The surroundings are very dignified and there are hundreds of little crevices to shelter in. And in Rome the summers are long and the sun shines all day.

Many of the cats were born from strays that mated and they have never been owned by a human being. They are totally free and can do whatever they like – but, of course, there's no fire to sit in front of in the long winter evenings, and no saucer of milk is ever put down by a loving owner.

Instead, they have to hunt

1 The ruins of the Forum in Rome are the 2,000-year-old home of an enormous colony of Wild Cats.

2 London's Wild Cats live on the bombed sites left over from the Second World War.

3 Mr Davis, who rescued the kittens, brought them along to the Blue Peter studio. He is convinced he has discovered an entirely new breed of cat, and has promised to bring *their* kittens to the studio, should Dennie and Ticky ever mate.

4 Dennie and Ticky – the two bombed site kittens – in their favourite hiding place – an old briefcase. You can see the strange markings showing quite clearly through Dennie's black hairs.

and it was then he made his discovery. One of the kittens appeared to be an entirely new breed of cat! At a distance, neither looked remarkable, one was black and one was piebald. But on closer inspection, Mr Davis found that the black one's coat was totally unlike any other he'd ever seen. Her guard hairs (the top layer of hairs on a cat's coat) were completely white, giving an almost striped appearance. And Mr Davis realised that as he had a male and a female kitten, if they mated they could produce an entirely new breed of cat.

We asked if the kittens could come to Blue Peter – and saw with our own eyes that what Mr Davis said was true. Dennie, the black kitten, really did have these unusual markings – and they showed particularly clearly on her black coat. It was possible that Ticky, the male kitten, also had these white hairs, but it was difficult to be sure because of his piebald coat.

We were amazed to find the kittens were so tame – Mr Davis said it had only taken them about two weeks to get used to their new home. Their favourite hiding-place was an old briefcase, and their favourite food was dehydrated fish coated with powdered milk.

Mr Davis promised that if Dennie and Ticky did have kittens, he'd bring them to show us on Blue Peter. And there's every chance that a mating will take place – Dennie and Ticky have gone to stay with cat expert Mrs Ashford of Kent. Mrs Ashford has already had one notable success in breeding the famous Curly-Coated Rex cats. She is the breeder of the first ever White Cornish Rex.

If all goes well – yet another new breed will have been discovered – thanks to Mr Davis and his bombed site rescue.

for their food, and every night they prowl amongst the ruins for rats, mice, and even the occasional lizard.

But there *is* someone who cares for the cats in the Forum. She's known as the Signora – and every day at five o'clock she walks to the Forum with a basket of food.

It's the only time they can really rely on getting something to eat, and every cat who lives in the Forum knows the Signora. They wait eagerly for her to arrive, and when she goes, a line of cats will accompany her all the way to the street, whilst the others watch and look forward to her return the following day.

We don't have any Roman remains in London as splendid as the Forum, but we still have bombed sites left over from the Second World War, and these

are where London's Wild Cats have made *their* homes. And – like the Signora – there's a devoted band of cat lovers who pay daily visits to the bombed sites to feed the cats. One regular visitor is Mr Davis of Streatham, and we were very excited when the 'phone rang in the Blue Peter Office and Mr Davis told us of his amazing new discovery.

On one of his feeding trips, a lady living in a house near to the bombed site asked if Mr Davis could catch four kittens she'd discovered in her disused cellar. Their mother was a bombed site wild cat who'd crept into the cellar for shelter – and the kittens were equally wild and had resisted all attempts to catch them. After several tries, Mr Davis was successful. He caught two of the kittens and took them home,

Paddington Gives a Service

A story by Michael Bond.
Illustrated by "Hargreaves"

"Cut to camera one."
"Stand by, two."
"Make sure Petra's O.K."
"Get ready to cue John."

Paddington's eyes, which had been unusually big all that day, grew larger still as he settled back in his seat and listened to the staccato commands rising up around him in the Blue Peter gallery.

Sitting at home watching the programme go out week after week, smoothly, with rarely a hint of crisis, it was indeed something of an eye-opener to be allowed in the "nerve-centre" while it actually happened.

Although he'd paid several visits to the studios in the past (and knew only too well that what the viewer saw was really only like the smooth and highly polished tip of a vast iceberg, with all sorts of other things going on behind the scenes), he'd never before been invited to sit in the holy of holies in order to watch a programme being put together, and he grew more and more excited as he felt tension inside the gallery mount.

It was like some mammoth jigsaw puzzle, but with the disadvantage that one piece in the wrong place and the whole structure was liable to fall apart.

On the far side of the darkened room stood an array of enormous television sets. Some relayed pictures from the various cameras down in the studio; others were set aside for viewing pieces of film to be shown later in the programme. Some had title captions; others were filled with what seemed to Paddington's eyes like meaningless shapes and patterns, though doubtless they all had a purpose.

Most important of all was a screen labelled TRANS-MISSION, which showed the picture being sent out to the viewers in their homes. Paddington was most impressed to think that not only were Mr and Mrs Brown, Jonathan and Judy, and Mrs Bird, seeing exactly the same picture back at number thirty-two Windsor Gardens, but that it was reaching ten million others as well.

In front of the monitor screens sat the director, and next to him the vision-mixer–changing the picture on the "transmission" screen at the press of a button. Beyond them were secretaries keeping a close eye on the timing of each item, the producer, the editor, a man in charge of all the technical equipment, and lots of other people too numerous to mention.

Paddington felt most important being a part of it all, for the man in charge of the gallery had said that visitors weren't normally allowed in at all during a transmission and that in all his experience it was the first time he could remember giving a bear permission.

If Paddington had any complaint at all it was that there was so much going on it was difficult to take it all in. He felt sure he wouldn't be able to remember half of it let alone explain the finer points when he next wrote a postcard to his Aunt Lucy in Peru, especially as he wasn't at all sure they had a radio in the Home for Retired Bears, let alone television.

In the end he decided to turn his attention to the view through a large double window on his left.

Beyond the batteries of lights which hung from the studio roof he could see the floor far below with its cameras gliding to and fro–some on pedestals, one on an enormous crane–and the microphone booms following Val, John and Peter's every move as they made their way to the next item on the programme, watched by waiting figures on the side–make-up girls, wardrobe men and women, scene men–in fact, a whole army of "backroom" workers.

The view held Paddington's full attention for some while and it wasn't until he saw the studio manager listen intently in his earphones for a moment and then begin making frantic signals in Peter's direction as he came to the end of an item on lighthouses, that he suddenly became aware of a change in the rhythm of the normally well-oiled "machinery" behind him, and as he turned back to the gallery his worst suspicions were confirmed.

Although the steady click-click as the vision-mixer changed pictures hadn't faltered, all was obviously not well.

Indeed, judging by the way the director was tearing his hair, he was in the middle of a crisis which needed to be solved pretty soon, otherwise he would finish the programme completely bald.

Paddington hesitated for a moment and then felt under his hat. Beneath the top, securely fastened by a piece of sticky tape, was a marmalade sandwich he kept for emergencies. From all that he could make out there was very much of an emergency taking place in the gallery at that very moment and he was about to offer his sandwich around when he stopped in his tracks.

"It's no good, we'll have to swop items," shouted the director into his microphone. "Get a message to Peter. Hold up a card or something . . . *anything*. Tell him Ivan Lobitov's gone into hiding. We'll do the item on boomerangs first and take it from there. Best of luck everyone."

Paddington nearly fell off his seat with alarm and indignation as he took in the words.

"Ivan Lobitov's *hiding*!" he exclaimed hotly. "I don't know what Mrs Bird's going to say."

Fortunately Paddington's voice was lost amid the babble which broke out on all sides as the director barked out a fresh series of orders to cover the situation, and after giving the row of screens in front of him several hard stares he slumped back into his seat again in order to consider the matter.

Ivan Lobitov was one of the leading tennis players behind the Iron Curtain, and having him on the programme had been something of a scoop for Blue Peter. In saying that Mrs Bird would be upset by the news of his non-appearance Paddington was merely scratching the surface, for the Browns' housekeeper was only one of countless followers of the game who'd been awaiting the event with eagerness.

Indeed, Paddington had been looking forward to it no end himself. Although he'd never actually played tennis he'd several times challenged Mr Brown to a game of ping-pong and it was largely as a result of a letter he'd laboriously penned to Blue Peter that the whole affair, including his invitation to the studio, had come about.

It had all begun some weeks before when John and Peter had started an intensive course with a well-known tennis coach, taking the viewers with them step by step along the way.

To celebrate their completing the course a full-size tennis court had been erected in the studio and the plan had been for Valerie to umpire a five-minute doubles match between Peter and "Boomerang" Barnes, the famous Australian player, on one side and John and Ivan Lobitov on the other.

Mr Lobitov had appeared earlier in the day for rehearsals and then retired to his dressing-room, seemingly in the best of spirits, in order to "rest". The news that he'd decided not to return to his own country and had gone into hiding for the time being was the kind of bombshell the staff of Blue Peter could well have done without in the middle of a programme, and Paddington's face grew longer and longer as one of the assistants filled in the details.

When she'd finished the girl read out a note of apology which had been found tucked beneath one of Mr Lobitov's racquets. In the normal course of events her words would have found a ready audience, but with problems arising every moment and time rapidly running out, she didn't exactly receive undivided attention.

Originally Peter had been going to introduce both guest players to the viewers after the match and invite Mr Barnes to demonstrate the boomerang from which he'd acquired his nickname.

As it was, the running order had been reversed and Peter had been left to do the item on his own *before* the match, leaving Valerie, John and Mr Barnes waiting anxiously on the court.

Now, despite frantic signals from the studio manager to make it last, even this desperate measure was coming to an end.

Another reason why the tale of woe didn't reach every ear was because one pair in particular had already left the gallery.

In fact, Paddington was already halfway down the stairs outside, and as he made his way along the corridor leading to the dressing-rooms he wore the kind of expression on his face that the Browns and Mrs Bird would have recognised immediately as boding ill for anyone who got in his way.

Fortunately for their peace of mind not even the miracle of television could penetrate the concrete walls surrounding the Television Centre, though as it happened their awareness of what was going on was to be delayed for only a minute or so, and for those left in the gallery there was even less time.

Paddington was a bear with a strong sense of right and wrong, and although he wasn't at all sure of what was going on, let alone why Mr Lobitov couldn't appear, he was determined to do something about the matter.

It was just as the director was about to send an urgent message through to the Presentation Department to say that the programme would be under-running by several minutes that his eye was caught by a rocking motion on one of the monitors as a cameraman tried to catch his attention.

"Good heavens!" he exclaimed. "What's that on camera one?"

For a few seconds everyone in the gallery watched in stunned silence as a strange-looking figure clad in a duffle-coat and hat and carrying a suitcase and tennis racquet crossed the studio and entered the court at the far end.

Then the director came to life again. With Peter winding up his talk on boomerangs and nothing else left to follow it was a time for quick decisions and he made one.

"I don't know what's going on," he said, "but whatever it is we'll take a chance."

"Stand by camera one."

"Cue Valerie. We're coming over to the tennis after all."

If Valerie was taken by surprise at the sudden turn of events it didn't show in her face. In fact, it was a masterpiece of controlled emotions, which was more than could be said for the occupants of number thirty-two Windsor Gardens at that moment as they crowded round their television set.

"Paddington!" exclaimed Jonathan and Judy together.

"What on earth's that bear up to now?" groaned Mrs Brown.

"And what on earth's he got on underneath his duffle-coat?" added Mr Brown, catching a brief glimpse of something white. "It looks like a table-cloth."

"I don't know," said Mrs Bird grimly, as Paddington bent down to make some last-minute adjustments to his attire, "but by the look of things we shall soon find out."

While Valerie had been introducing the item from the top of her umpire's stand Peter had made a quick change into his tennis clothes and by the time she'd presented "Boomerang" Barnes to the viewers he was in place beside Paddington.

"Shall I take your duffle-coat?" he asked politely. "You may find it a bit hot under the lights."

Paddington considered the matter for a moment. Now that he was actually in the studio he was beginning to wish he'd had time to look for a few safety pins, or even not bothered with Mr

Lobitov's shorts at all, for they felt distinctly large and uncomfortable.

"No, thank you, Mr Purves," he announced at last. "I may have an accident if you do!"

"In that case," said Valerie hastily, "perhaps we'd better start. Mr Barnes to serve."

The words were hardly out of her mouth when a sound like a pistol shot rang round the studio.

"Are you all right, Mr Brown?" asked Peter, helping Paddington to his feet and pointing him in the right direction as he replaced his hat for him.

"I think so," gasped Paddington. "I'm not quite sure."

Although he knew Mr Barnes was called "Boomerang" because of his quick returns Paddington hadn't expected the first one to be made via his head and he directed a hard stare across the net at his opponent.

"Fifteen love," called Valerie.

"Er . . . thank you, dear," replied Paddington, looking rather surprised that Miss Singleton was being unusually familiar.

The next few minutes seemed like a dream. Paddington was vaguely aware of figures in white dashing to and fro across his vision. As far as he could make out Mr Barnes's serves were even more deadly than his famous returns. Several times the ball passed perilously close to him as Peter made valiant efforts to save the game and he was glad when at long last he heard Valerie announce that refreshments were ready.

"Thank you very much, Miss Singleton," he called, as he hurried across to the side-line. "I'd like an orange squash, please."

Playing tennis was obviously thirsty work at the best of times, but when it involved playing against someone like "Boomerang" Barnes *and* wearing a duffle-coat into the bargain it was even worse and he was looking forward to a break in the proceedings.

"I'm afraid I don't mean that sort of *juice*," explained Valerie. "It's a French word. *Deuce*. It means the score's forty all."

Paddington looked most disappointed. "*Forty all!*" he exclaimed, hardly able to believe his ears. "But I've only touched the ball once!"

"Advantage Barnes and Noakes," called Valerie, as the ball whistled past his right ear.

"Fancy using French," continued Paddington bitterly, addressing the world in general as the ball whistled past his left ear.

"Game Barnes and Noakes," called Valerie. "Paddington to serve. And we'd better make it quick," she continued. "Time's running out."

Swallowing his indignation, Paddington bent down to gather up a pile of balls in a corner near his suitcase. As he did so a strange expression came over his face. Something about the feel of his shorts made him realise that standing up again, let alone doing any sort of moving about on the court, was going to need a great deal of care indeed. That apart, picking up two balls was bad enough, but trying to grasp four or five at the same time–as "Boomerang" Barnes did with such apparent ease–was well nigh impossible with paws.

Paddington struggled for a moment or two and then, conscious of a note of urgency in Valerie's voice, as she called for the game to begin, and the sight of a man wearing headphones gesticulating in the direction of the studio clock, he came to a decision. Bending low over his suitcase, he spent the next few moments doing something mysterious to his racquet.

When he did finally stand a gasp went round the studio, for without moving from the spot Paddington raised his racquet and the ball fairly hurtled across the court, rebounded from the floor, struck Mr Barnes a glancing blow on the chest, and then shot back across the net.

If Paddington paused in order to take aim again it was missed by the vast majority of the onlookers, and almost before Valerie had time to call out the score the process had been repeated.

"Thirty love!" shouted Valerie.

"Good work!" called Peter. "Keep it up!"

But there was no need for words of encouragement, for Paddington not only looked as if he could keep going all night—he gave the appearance of being unable to help it.

"Forty love!" shouted Valerie. She was about to add "Advantage to Paddington and Purves", but it was too late. With a twang which set the studio ablaze with excitement the game came to an end and Peter was pumping Paddington's paw up and down like a yo-yo.

"Boy, what a combination," cried John as he and "Boomerang" Barnes leapt the net in order to offer their congratulations to the winning pair.

"One game each," said Valerie. "And I think that's a very fair result."

"Here, here," agreed John. "By golly, I wasn't looking forward to playing against Ivan Lobitov, but I reckon Ivan Paddington's twice as good. You must have been putting in a bit of practice on the Steppes."

"Oh, no," said Paddington earnestly. "But I've had one or two goes in Mr Brown's garage."

"I knew it!" Mr Brown jumped up and peered at his television screen. "He's been using the ball from my tennis trainer—the one with the elastic on. I usually hang it from the garage beam. I wondered where it had got to. He must have tied it to his racquet."

"Ssh!" said Mrs Brown. "I think Mr Barnes is trying to say something."

"He's giving Paddington his boomerang," cried Jonathan. "Gosh! That's jolly sporting. Lucky beggar!"

"I know one thing," said Judy, as the rest of the cast gathered round to applaud, "he couldn't give it to a better person. Paddington'll think it's very good value. That's one thing he'll never be able to throw away."

As a chorus of groans mingled with the closing music of Blue Peter Mrs Brown stood up and glanced at the clock.

"Isn't it clever," she said, "how they always manage to finish the programme dead on time."

"It's not only clever," said Mr Brown, for once, but all unknowingly, doing the figure on the screen a grave injustice, "with Paddington around it's a miracle!"

HARGREAVES

Jumbo Jet
Giant of the Skies

"Jumbo", the Boeing 747, is the world's largest and fastest jetliner in regular passenger service. It is not just a scaled-up version of the earlier Boeing 707, but an entirely new aircraft specially designed for high-speed heavy-load duties. But in spite of its massiveness, the Jumbo can land and take off in less space than many jetliners less than half its size! Why is the Jumbo so big? The answer is simple. In the next five years, the number of people wanting to travel by air will have doubled. Busy airports will not be able to cope with all the extra normal-size aircraft that would be needed to carry them, so a giant aircraft had to be designed. The result was – JUMBO.

Vickers Super VC.10. Length 171 feet 8 inches; cruising speed 570 m.p.h. 137 passengers.

Boeing 707. Length 152 feet 11 inches; cruising speed 580 m.p.h.; 159 passengers.

Boeing 747. The Jumbo. Length 231 feet 4 inches cruising speed 625 m.p.h. 490 passengers.

Longer, fatter, faster than its companions – no wonder it's called "Jumbo"!

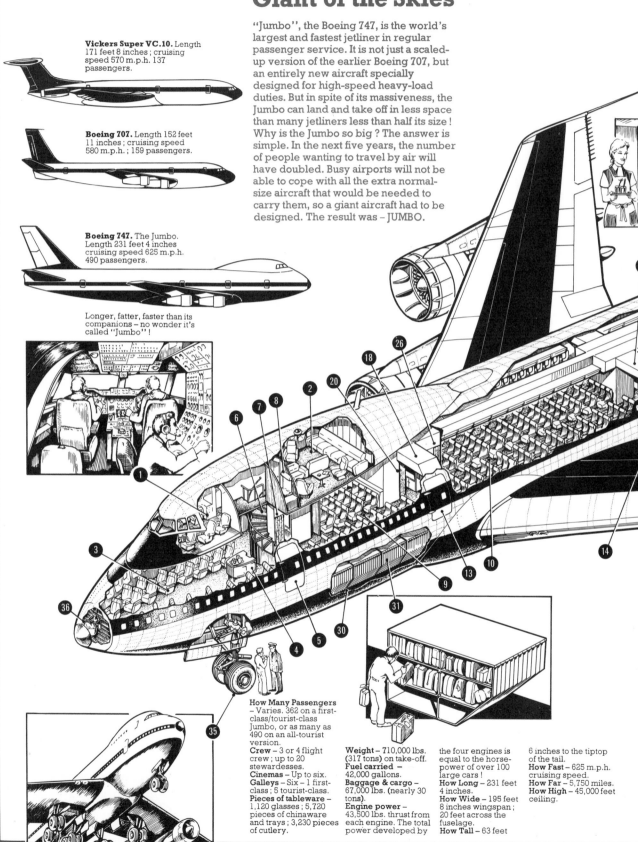

How Many Passengers – Varies. 362 on a first-class/tourist-class Jumbo, or as many as 490 on an all-tourist version.

Crew – 3 or 4 flight crew; up to 20 stewardesses.

Cinemas – Up to six.

Galleys – Six – 1 first-class; 5 tourist-class.

Pieces of tableware – 1,120 glasses; 5,720 pieces of chinaware and trays; 3,230 pieces of cutlery.

Weight – 710,000 lbs. (317 tons) on take-off.

Fuel carried – 42,000 gallons.

Baggage & cargo – 67,000 lbs. (nearly 30 tons).

Engine power – 43,500 lbs. thrust from each engine. The total power developed by the four engines is equal to the horse-power of over 100 large cars!

How Long – 231 feet 4 inches.

How Wide – 195 feet 8 inches wingspan; 20 feet across the fuselage.

How Tall – 63 feet 6 inches to the tiptop of the tail.

How Fast – 625 m.p.h. cruising speed.

How Far – 5,750 miles.

How High – 45,000 feet ceiling.

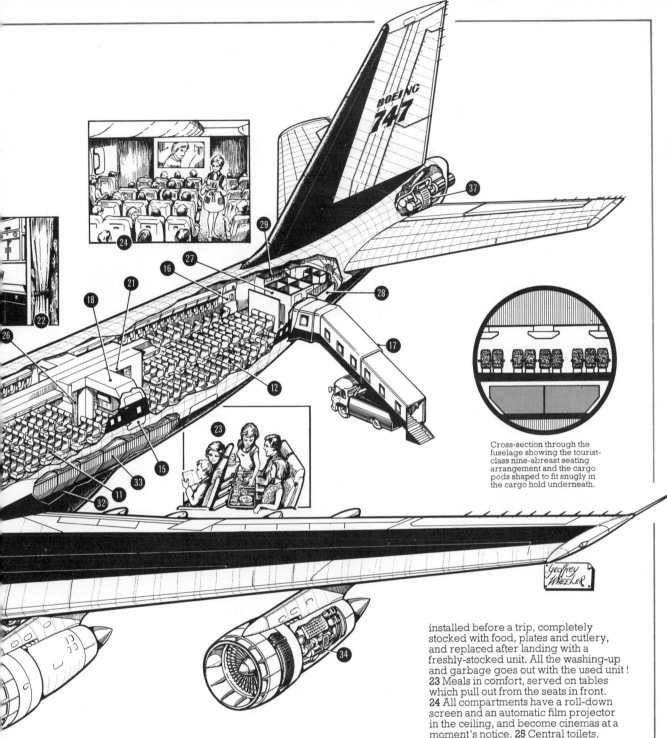

Cross-section through the fuselage showing the tourist-class nine-abreast seating arrangement and the cargo pods shaped to fit snugly in the cargo hold underneath.

Key to numbers

1 Flight Deck – the "driving position" and nerve centre from which the aircraft is controlled. Captain, co-pilot and engineer make up the flight crew. A fourth member, an observer, is carried in some aircraft. 2 "Penthouse" luxury lounge for first-class passengers. 3 First-class saloon. 4 Coffee and cocktail bar. 5 Passenger door to first-class accommodation. 6 Spiral staircase between saloon and lounge. 7 Single galley unit serving meals for first-class passengers. 8 First-class toilet. 9 10 11 12 Main-deck tourist-class accommodation, divided into compartments to give passengers the feeling of being in

smaller cabins rather than one long tunnel. Seats are arranged nine-abreast (see Cross-Section Diagram) but they can be fitted ten-abreast to increase seating capacity. 13 14 15 16 Tourist-class passenger doors, on both sides of aircraft. 17 Mobile telescopic passenger staircase that adjusts to the height of any of the passenger doors – just one of the many pieces of special equipment that serve the "Jumbo". 18 Emergency lockers containing life-saving equipment over all passenger doors. 19 Pull-out overhead trays for hand luggage. 20 Double galley unit. 21 Triple galley unit. 22 Detail of a galley unit. Units are

installed before a trip, completely stocked with food, plates and cutlery, and replaced after landing with a freshly-stocked unit. All the washing-up and garbage goes out with the used unit ! 23 Meals in comfort, served on tables which pull out from the seats in front. 24 All compartments have a roll-down screen and an automatic film projector in the ceiling, and become cinemas at a moment's notice. 25 Central toilets. 26 Wardrobes for passengers' topcoats. 27 Rear toilets. 28 Stewardesses' wardrobe. 29 Passengers' wardrobe. 30 Baggage hold. 31 Baggage is carried in special containers or "pods" for quicker loading and unloading. 32 Cargo hold. 33 Cargo pods. 34 Power plants – four enormous Pratt & Whitney JT9D-3 jet engines. 35 Undercarriage. The Jumbo rolls on no fewer than 18 wheels – four sets of four-wheel bogies and a twin nose-wheel, all of which fold away in flight. 36 Radar scanner. 37 Auxiliary Power Unit, generating electricity when the aircraft is on the ground and supplying power to such items as lights and vacuum cleaners as the ground staff prepare for the next flight.

Mystery Picture

Colour the spaces as indicated by the numbers and the picture will appear.

1 Dark Brown
2 Black 3 Blue
4 Light Brown
5 Yellow 6 Green

BLUE PETER OLD
PEOPLE'S BUS

Have you ever thought what it must be like to be lonely – really lonely all the time, I mean? If you're reading this book, it's ten to one you're with your family or your friends, and you might think it would be quite nice to be on your own once in a while. But this year we discovered that there are two million old people living in Britain who are on their own *all* the time!

I went to visit an old lady called Mrs Abbot who lives just round the corner from the Blue Peter Studio, and she hadn't been out of the house for five years. But she wasn't miserable and sorry for herself. She was very brave and cheerful, and she told me that it was because she's almost blind that she doesn't dare go out into the street. All her old friends have died, there's no one left to take her out, and visitors are very rare. A home-help comes for an hour each day to bring her food, and see to her needs, but when the home-help closes the door, there's nothing left for Mrs Abbot but silence.

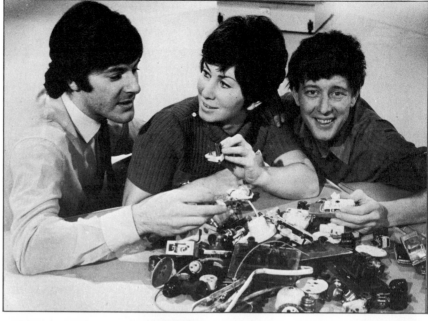

As we chatted together, I thought what a remarkable old lady she was. If I'd been shut up on my own for five weeks, I'd be feeling pretty sorry for myself, but five years. . . .

Some old people are a lot worse off than Mrs Abbot, but others are able to get out occasionally. Special buses equipped with lifts for wheel-chairs call regularly at old people's homes to take them to places called Day Centres, where they can have a meal and a chat, and make friends with other people.

The trouble is that there aren't nearly enough special buses to go round; so that's why we decided to ask *you* to provide a Blue Peter Old People's Bus.

We thought we'd ask you to make a great sacrifice. We knew we could raise enough money to buy the Blue Peter Old People's Bus if you gave up your old metal toy cars to be melted down. We knew we were asking a lot, but we also knew that you wouldn't let us down ! And as well as old toy cars, we asked for old electric light plugs and fittings because the brass inside them was also valuable as scrap metal.

A great warehouse was rented in the City of London to act as a collecting depot, and soon your parcels began to arrive. Thousands and thousands of old cars of every shape and size, and enough electric light plugs to illuminate the whole of London !

On December 29th we were able to announce that you'd done it again ! You sent us enough scrap metal to provide not only an Old People's Bus, but also :
10 baths with lever taps
12 high-backed armchairs

6 ejector seats
4 refrigerators
3 television sets
1 battery-operated wheelchair

A marvellous result, but there was more to come. Cars and plugs were still pouring in, and with them came agonised letters from collectors of antique toys :

''Do you realise that every day you may be throwing price-less collector's pieces into the blast furnace ?''

No, to be perfectly honest, we didn't, but the moment we heard, we stopped all ship-ments to the furnace and called the experts in. The collectors rallied round and helped us to sort out hundreds of potentially valuable items from the millions of cars that were still pouring in to the depot.

It was then that we decided to hold a Blue Peter Auction.

We didn't know very much about antique toy cars, but we knew even less about how to hold an auction.

So John went to Phillips Son

There are two million old people in Britain who live alone all the time. We asked you to send all your old toy cars and electric light plugs so that we could buy a bus to take them to a Day Centre where they could meet their friends. Soon our collecting depot was bulging with millions of cars and plugs...

& Neale – the famous auction-eers – to find out how it was done. He spent a day as an auction-room porter and watched Mr Hawkins, the Chief Auctioneer, at work.

On Tuesday, February 24th, with John looking very nervous in a smart suit and tie, we held our Blue Peter Car Auction.

Peter was the auction-room porter this time, which meant holding up each lot as Auction-eer Noakes gave the description and then shouting ''Showing here !'' so that the buyers would know what they were bidding for.

John started off very hesi-tantly (he admitted afterwards

that he was terrified!) but soon he looked as though he'd been an auctioneer all his life.

"Twenty pounds I'm bid for this magnificent box of buses. Twenty-one, twenty-two, twenty-three in the window, twenty-four by the door – it's against you, sir. Are you done at twenty-four – bang!''

Every time the mallet fell, our chances of buying yet another Blue Peter Bus increased, and by the end of the day, John was able to announce that the sale had raised £746.

On Monday, March 9th, we made our final announcement. When everything had been added together, all the money from the plugs and the toys together with the £746 and all the cheques and Postal Orders that had been sent to the Blue Peter office, the grand total was:
4 Old People's Buses
2 battery-operated wheel chairs
40 special high-backed chairs

15 low baths with lever taps
15 mini refrigerators
6 television sets
18 ejector seats

The buses would provide a release from loneliness for hundreds of old people, and the other things would certainly make their lives easier and more comfortable.

We said thank you on the programme, but one of the nicest things about the Blue Peter Book is that it makes it possible for us to say *thank you* again – but this time it's written down in print forever.

We sorted out all the valuable cars and held an auction which raised £746. When all the money was added together, we had enough for *four* Old People's Buses, 2 electric wheel chairs, 40 high-backed chairs, 15 baths, 15 refrigerators, 6 television sets and 18 ejector seats.

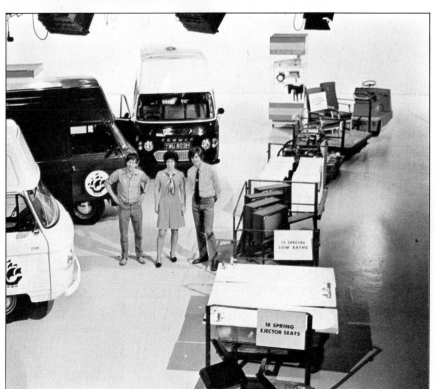

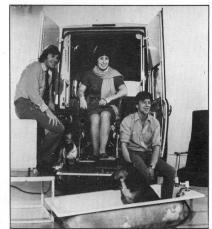

The Man in White

On a summer's day in 1864, a man in a white suit was driving in his coach through Italy on his way to see the Emperor of the French. On that journey, something happened that was to change not only his own life, but the lives of millions of people all over the world. The man was Henri Dunant, a banker from Switzerland, and this is his story.

Bob Broomfield.

1 When Henri Dunant came to a village called Solferino, his road was blocked by French soldiers. "I've come to see the Emperor," he cried. "Let me pass!"

2 "No!" cried an officer. "The Emperor is leading his armies against the Austrians. Any moment the battle will start. You must go back at once!" But Henri Dunant took a

3 horse and rode after the marching soldiers. He'd never seen a battle and he thought it would be exciting. Soon he reached the battlefield and saw

4 the Austrian Army standing in closed ranks with the shining Imperial Eagles glinting above them, and

5 galloping towards them came the French lancers and dragoons with the sun glinting down on their gaily coloured uniforms.

6 Dunant looked down on the glittering scene. "What a splendid sight," he thought. But then the armies

7 met head on and he watched in horror as thousands of men fought to the death. The shouts and the blinding gun smoke were horrifying. Hours later

8 Dunant walked through the silent battlefield. The Austrians had fled, and dead and dying men lay everywhere. There were no ambulances, no doctors and no nurses.

9 Back in Solferino he watched as the wounded French soldiers came limping in. Some of them could hardly stand, but no-one came to help them. Henri Dunant decided to take charge. He

10 gave all his money to some men to buy medicines and bandages in a nearby town. He had the

11 wounded soldiers taken to the village church, and organised the village women to give them water to drink and to wash their wounds.

12 The soldiers called Dunant the Man in White, for though his suit was crumpled now, and dirty, he was easy to pick out as he helped the wounded soldiers. Then

13 two men in Austrian uniform came to the Church door. "Throw them out," called the French soldiers. "They're enemies!" But

14 Henri Dunant treated them as kindly as if they were French. "We are all brothers here," he said.

15 After the war, he wrote a book about the sufferings of the wounded men on both sides. The book was read all over the world.

16 Soon men from fourteen countries came to Switzerland to hear Dunant tell what should be done. "In a war, we must have doctors and nurses and ambulances who will help the wounded on both sides. And there must be a sign for help that everyone will recognise."

17 "The Swiss Flag" suggested one doctor at the meeting. "Change that and make it a red cross on a white ground."

18 "Splendid!" said Dunant. "Make the Red Cross the sign of humanity and kindness and help to the wounded. Let the Red Cross remind men of all countries that we are brothers."

Bengo

Three stories
without words
by Tim

It was half past eight on the evening of Saturday, the 7th of February. The place: the National Hall of Olympia, London. The occasion: the final moments before the announcement of the Supreme Champion at Cruft's Dog Show, 1970.

I was in the arena with photographers and reporters from every important newspaper and television company in Britain.

The rules at Cruft's for Press men are that all reporters must stay at the side of the arena until top Judge, Stanley Dangerfield, has made his announcement. Then, at a signal from one of the Stewards, everybody runs like mad to the platform to get the first pictures of the year's Supreme Champion. Photographs first – interviews later.

For the last two days, 8,397 dogs had been inspected and judged, more than a hundred had already been selected and declared "best in breed", and now, at last, the best of best, the Supreme Champion, was going to be chosen.

Stanley Dangerfield approached each dog in turn, and inspected its face, its quarters, its coat, and looked keenly at the way it moved. At the side of the arena we loaded our cameras and checked our lenses while Stanley's meticulous inspection went on. I didn't envy him his job! Every dog was a superb specimen of its breed. At last he patted a frisky little poodle on the head and stepped up to the microphone:

"Ladies and Gentlemen . . ." Suddenly all the talking stopped and the cameramen looked like greyhounds in the slips.

"The year's Supreme Champion at Cruft's is Grant, the Pyrenean Mountain Dog owned by Mr Prince."

There was a thunderous roar of applause as Mr Prince and his magnificent dog leapt up on to the platform. Then, the pretty Princess Margarethe of Sweden stepped forward smiling, and holding with both hands the great silver trophy which is the most coveted award in the world of dogs.

didn't know what had hit him. Then, taking a deep breath and gathering up all my courage, I stepped forward with the microphone.

"Mr Prince, I'd like to invite you to be on 'Blue Peter' on Monday at five to five."

"Interviews after the pictures, mate,"growled a Press photographer beside me.

"O.K.," I said, and stepped back again with the knowledge

For two days, top dogs from all over the country parade before the judges.

I jostled for position with the world's Press photographers to get shots of the Supreme Champion.

The next moment I was belting across the arena with all the other reporters – like a pack of hounds at full cry. I had two stills cameras round my neck and a microphone in my hand, and panting down my neck were the "Blue Peter" film cameraman, sound recordist and Director. Everybody ran hard, but the "Blue Peter" team arrived at the platform seconds before the others.

The Press photographers clicked and flashed away and the film cameras whirred all around me. On the platform, the beautifully gleaming white champion seemed to be thoroughly enjoying it all, but his master looked as though he

that I'd got the biggest scoop in the dog world for ''Blue Peter'' !

My assignment had started at 6 o'clock in the morning, 48 hours before the Supreme Champion was announced. I was there to photograph the dogs as they arrived, and to try to interview their owners.

Before dawn, dogs of all shapes and sizes started to arrive, and as soon as they were inside the Hall, frantic last-minute titivations began. The St Bernards were given bibs to stop them from slavering on their chests.

I don't know why it is, but there's something very funny about a lot of dogs of different shapes and sizes all together. The road outside Olympia was an explosion of yapping, yelping and panting dogs. Frisky terriers bounded out of ''minis'' while stately Salukis lolled languidly in limousines, sophisticated poodles tripped out of taxis, and gun dogs slavered in the backs of shooting brakes.

Some of their owners must have been up all night polishing and brushing and combing them for this, the biggest dog event of the year, and they were determined that all their hard work wasn't going to be undone by an unlucky shower of rain.

One pair of poodles looked as though they were wearing pyjamas. I knew it was early in the morning, but even so . . . !

Several of the dogs had rubber boots, and one lady who said she couldn't afford boots had tied little plastic bags round each foot of her Borzoi hunting-dog.

I met a fellow from Birmingham who looked as though he was wearing one of those way-out shaggy sheepskin jackets, but on closer inspection, it turned out to be a great big Afghan Hound slung round his shoulders. The owner didn't have any boots or even plastic bags, but he was equally determined not to get his dog's feet wet.

There were poodles in curlers, terriers in towelling jackets, and great sad-eyed St Bernards wearing bibs to stop them slavering on their newly groomed coats.

I wonder how different it looked in 1886 when the first dog show was held in Westminster. That show was only for terriers whose owners had been brought together by an enterprising young dog-biscuit salesman named Charles Cruft. The show was such a success that within five years, dogs of different breeds were travelling from all over the world to the famous Cruft's Dog Show.

In those days, the biggest attraction was the dogs owned by famous people. Queen Victoria, a great dog lover, arranged for her pets to be seen at Cruft's. Her son, the Prince of Wales, who was a keen sportsman, sent his finest gun dogs, but the most exotic of them all was a leash of Borzois, the Russian hunting-dogs, sent by His Imperial Majesty, the Tsar of Russia.

Charles Cruft lived to be 87, and by the end of his life the Dog Shows had become a National Institution as they are to this day. But the strange thing is that throughout his long life, Charles Cruft never owned a dog !

CRUFT'S DOG SHOW AT THE ROYAL AGRICULTURAL HALL: WINNERS OF CHAMPIONSHIPS.

MR. R. LEADBETTER'S MASTIFF, "MARCELLA." — MR. K. MCDOUALL'S ENGLISH SETTER, "LOGAN MODEL." — MESSRS. ISMAN AND WALMSLEY'S ST. BERNARD, "JUDITH ISMAN."
MR. S. MANGIN'S BLOODHOUND, "HORDLE HERCULES." — MR. J. FARROW'S COCKER SPANIEL, "SANDY OBO." — MRS. P. SHEWELL'S IRISH WOLFHOUND, "COTSWOLD."
MR. R. TAIT'S COLLIE, "WISHAW-CLINKER." — MR. J. J. HOLGATE'S IRISH WATER SPANIEL, "PATSEY BOYLE." — MR. H. R. COOKE'S FLAT-COATED RETRIEVER, "BLACK QUILL."
MR. F. W. SMITH'S CLUMBER SPANIEL, "GORSE OF AUCHENTORLIE." — MRS. M. MANLEY'S BULLDOG, "EVELYN DUCHESS."

Mystery Babies Competition

How good are you at recognising famous people and what they looked like when they were babies? These babies all grew up to be well known, so if you can guess who they are and pair the photographs together, turn to page 77 for details of our Blue Peter Competition.

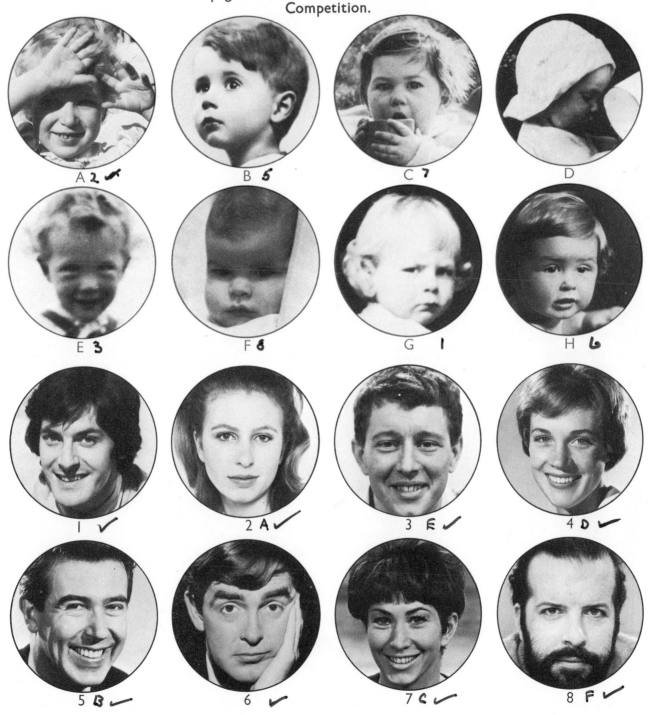

A 2 ✓   B 5   C 7   D

E 3   F 8   G 1   H 6

1 ✓   2 A ✓   3 E ✓   4 D ✓

5 B ✓   6 ✓   7 C ✓   8 F ✓

Answers

Puzzle Pictures

1 *Saltmarsh Silvercrest—a* champion Percheron stallion and the heaviest horse in Britain. Saltmarsh weighs 2,772 lbs. and at 18.1 hands high we needed a step-ladder to mount him.

2 A *"Blower" Bentley* and an identical "do-it-yourself" glass-fibre kit model.

3 *Pipe Major Ramsey* of the Irish Guards gives John a never-to-be-forgotten bagpipe lesson!

4 At *Expo 70,* this *20-foot balloon,* which took $2\frac{1}{2}$ hours to pump full of air, floated 150 feet above the British Pavilion.

5 *Learning how to be the back legs of a pantomime horse.* The costumes were made by Bob Clemens (inside Tom the Cat). Peter was the horse's front legs.

6 The *world's biggest potted chrysanthemum* and a normal-sized plant. Mr Blythe, who grew the "giant," had to dismantle his greenhouse before he could take it by lorry to the Horticultural Hall, Westminster.

7 Log Chopping with Bob Singleton, a British contender in the *World Log Chopping Championships.*

8 This *Self-inflating Escape Chute* is used as a method of rescuing passengers from burning 'planes that have just landed or are about to take off.

9 *Restoring the Blue Peter* at British Rail's Doncaster workshops. She has been painted in LNER apple green with LNER on the tender.

10 *Harry Morris,* the BBC's ace sound effects operator, showed us how to make home-made rain, horse's hooves, and creaking door noises.

11 Brigadier Clapham, Sergeant at Arms & Common Crier, with the *Lord Mayor of London's Mace.* The silvergilt mace was made in 1735 and the decorations include coat of arms of the City.

12 We help *Robert Harbin,* the world-famous Illusionist, to perform a complicated trick with Val.

13 *The Royal Canadian Mounted Police,* led by Staff Sergeants Cave and Wing, demonstrated their lance drill in the Blue Peter Studio.

The Case of the Green Panda

1 & 2 Sims said the cage must be heated because pandas come from the tropical jungles of Tibet. Pandas are found only in the mountains of Northern China, and anyway, there are no jungles in Tibet. Count two mistakes if you spotted this.

3 There are only two pandas in captivity in Europe–Chi-Chi in London, and An-An in Moscow. There are no pandas in Basle Zoo.

4 Bamboo shoots are a panda's staple diet and are certainly not poisonous to them.

5 Mount Fujiyama is in Japan and not China where pandas come from.

6 China is a People's Republic and is not ruled by an Emperor.

Biddy Baxter, Edward Barnes and Rosemary Gill would like to acknowledge the help of Gillian Farnsworth and Margaret Parnell

Designed by Haydon Young

Useful Information

Donald Jackson: 28 Grove Lane, London S.E.5. (The other scribe who writes for the Queen is Dorothy Hutton, MVO)

Grahame Dangerfield: Four Limes, Wheathampstead, Hertfordshire.

Cruft's: c/o The Kennel Club, 1 Clarges Street, London W.1.

British Red Cross Society: 6 Grosvenor Crescent, London S.W.1.

Daniel Lambert: Newarke Houses Museum, Leicester.

How to win a "Blue Peter" badge: By sending us interesting letters/ good ideas for the programme/ drawings/paintings/models that have been particularly well made/ and competitions.

"Blue Peter" Mini Books:
Book of Television
Book of Teddy's Clothes
Book of Pets
Safari to Morocco
Expedition to Ceylon
Book of Presents
Book of Daniel
Book of Guide Dogs

Acknowledgements

All the photographs in this book were taken by Charles E. Walls with the exception of the following: No. 5 of the Puzzle Pictures (page 4) and wild cats (page 53) by permission of Andrzej Slezak; Holbein Portrait (page 14) by Walker Art Gallery, Liverpool; Investiture (page 17) by Barratts; Daniel Lambert portrait and cartoon (page 23) by Leicester Museum & Art Gallery; Gad's Hill House (page 36), Dickens at his desk (page 37), Cat on London bomb-site (page 52), and Cruft's Dog Show (page 74) by Radio Times Hulton Picture Library; Blacking factory (page 36) by Dickens Fellowship; Stilt Fishing (page 41) by Gamini Jaysinghe; Forum (page 52) by Barnaby's Picture Library. "A Very Queer Small Boy" was written by Dorothy Smith. "The Man in White" was illustrated by Robert Broomfield; Bengo, Bleep and Booster and the Mystery Picture by "Tim"; "The Case of the Green Panda" was illustrated by Bernard Blatch, and Dickens as a boy was drawn by Robert Broomfield.

Blue Peter Competition

Would you like to meet Valerie, John, Peter and the rest of the "Blue Peter" team? Would you like to see all the animals? Would you like to come to London and have tea with them all? This is your chance!

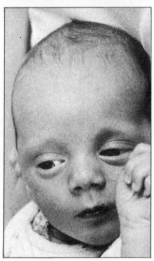 

Daniel 6 *weeks*   *Daniel* 13 *months*

Look at these pictures of Daniel, our "Blue Peter" baby, and see how he's changed in 12 months. On page 75 you'll find some more babies with

photographs of what they look like now they've grown up. We want you to guess who the grown-ups are, and which is their baby photograph. Write this on a piece of paper like this (we've done the first one for you to show you what to do):

Name	Baby Photo	Adult Photo
Peter Purves	G	1

Carry on like this until you have a list of all eight personalities. Send your answers together with your entry form to: Blue Peter Competition, BBC Television Centre, London W.12.

The First Prize will be an invitation to an exciting

Blue Peter Party

and there will be lots of competition badges for the runners-up, too.

First Prize winners and runners-up will be notified by letter. The closing date for entries is 11th January 1971.

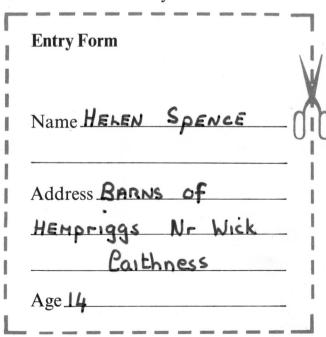

Entry Form

Name HELEN SPENCE

Address BARNS of HEMpriggs Nr Wick Caithness

Age 14

First published 1970. Published by the British Broadcasting Corporation,
35 Marylebone High Street, London W1M 4AA.
SBN 563 09398 6 Printed in England by Sir Joseph Causton & Sons Ltd.
London and Eastleigh